IMAGES OF \

C000255069

# THE AMERICANS ON D-DAY AND IN NORMANDY

## RARE PHOTOGRAPHS FROM WARTIME ARCHIVES

### Brooke Blades

Pen & Sword
**MILITARY**

First published in Great Britain in 2019 by
**PEN & SWORD MILITARY**
An imprint of
Pen & Sword Books Ltd
47 Church Street
Barnsley
South Yorkshire
S70 2AS

ISBN 978-1-52674-396-1

Typeset by Concept, Huddersfield, West Yorkshire HD4 5JL
Printed and bound in the UK by CPI Group (UK) Ltd, Croydon, CR0 4YY

Pen & Sword Books Limited incorporates the imprints of Atlas, Archaeology, Aviation, Discovery, Family History, Fiction, History, Maritime, Military, Military Classics, Politics, Select, Transport, True Crime, Air World, Frontline Publishing, Leo Cooper, Remember When, Seaforth Publishing, The Praetorian Press, Wharncliffe Local History, Wharncliffe Transport, Wharncliffe True Crime and White Owl.

For a complete list of Pen & Sword titles please contact
PEN & SWORD BOOKS LIMITED
47 Church Street, Barnsley, South Yorkshire S70 2AS, England
E-mail: enquiries@pen-and-sword.co.uk
Website: www.pen-and-sword.co.uk

# Contents

**Acknowledgements** . . . . . . . . . . . . . . . . . . . . . . . . . . **5**

**Introduction** . . . . . . . . . . . . . . . . . . . . . . . . . . **7**

Chapter One

**Preparations in England** . . . . . . . . . . . . . . . . . . **11**

Chapter Two

**Airborne Landings on the Cotentin Peninsula** . . . . . . . **23**

Map: Airborne Landings on the Cotentin . . . . . . . . . . . . . . . . . . . . 24

Map: Merderet Causeway Crossing, 9 June 1944 . . . . . . . . . . . . . . . . 27

Map: Carentan Causeway Crossing, 11 June 1944 . . . . . . . . . . . . . . . 29

Map: AMS Sainte-Mère-Église 1944 . . . . . . . . . . . . . . . . . . . . . . 36

Chapter Three

**Landings on Easy Red and Fox Green Beaches** . . . . . . . **53**

Map: Early Landings on and Advance from Eastern End of Omaha Beach . . 54

Chapter Four

**The Photographs of Sergeant Richard Taylor** . . . . . . . . **66**

Chapter Five

**Beach Landings and Views** . . . . . . . . . . . . . . . . . . **78**

Map: Early Landings on and Advance from Western End of Omaha Beach . 79

Map: Early Landings on Dog White Sector . . . . . . . . . . . . . . . . . . 82

Map: Entry into Vierville . . . . . . . . . . . . . . . . . . . . . . . . . . . . . 83

Map: Early Landings on and Advance Inland near Les Moulins . . . . . . . . 85

Chapter Six

**Utah Beach and Coastal Defences** . . . . . . . . . . . . . . **103**

Chapter Seven

**Soldiers, Prisoners and Civilians** . . . . . . . . . . . . . . **114**

Chapter Eight

**Advance to Cherbourg and Interior to Saint-Lô** . . . . . . . **146**

Map: Normandy from Beaches to Avranches . . . . . . . . . . . . . . . . . 147

Chapter Nine

**The Wounded** . . . . . . . . . . . . . . . . . . . . . . . . . . **181**

Chapter Ten

**The Dead and Their Cemeteries** . . . . . . . . . . . . . . **202**

Chapter Eleven

**Then, Now and Then** . . . . . . . . . . . . . . . . . . . . . **227**

Map: Colleville . . . . . . . . . . . . . . . . . . . . . . . . . . . 230

Map: St Laurent . . . . . . . . . . . . . . . . . . . . . . . . . . 232

Map: Vierville . . . . . . . . . . . . . . . . . . . . . . . . . . . . 234

**Image Credits** . . . . . . . . . . . . . . . . . . . . . . . . . **244**

**Notes** . . . . . . . . . . . . . . . . . . . . . . . . . . . . . . . **247**

**References** . . . . . . . . . . . . . . . . . . . . . . . . . . . **250**

# Acknowledgements

No research is undertaken without the assistance of others nor is any writing emerging from that research the sole product of one person. It is therefore a sincere pleasure to express my appreciation to the friends, former colleagues and archives staff who have been instrumental in the preparation of this volume.

Rick Wherley gave me many books. Rick has always been eager to talk about Normandy and discuss the past as if it was the present. Phil Pendleton participated in early concept discussions of a Normandy study. John Lawrence and Richard Baublitz provided encouragement along the way; John kindly donated some important recent literature to the cause. Jason Vendetti showed sustained interest and enabled Julie Cressman to produce most of the maps in the volume. Frank Dunsmore produced another map and was always willing to see the latest photographs from the National Archives. To Georges Augustins and Jehanne Féblot-Augustins, many thanks for their research assistance and friendship.

Henry Wilson at Pen & Sword Books Ltd was an early supporter of this volume and the concept of combining thematic photographic essays with text. I thank him for his pleasant and professional manner. Many hands at Pen & Sword were involved in the production of this volume, particularly those belonging to Barnaby Blacker, Katie Eaton, Lori Jones and Matt Jones.

Lieutenant Colonel Michael Perry (ret.), the executive director of the Army Heritage Center Foundation in Carlisle, has a deeply personal interest in the D-Day landings. Mike sustained the research in numerous ways, including providing access to his father's papers and photographs. Sarah Pendleton and Lori Wheeler at the Military History Institute Library in Carlisle provided assistance with images from the S.L.A. Marshall Collection. Bernard Lebrec in Normandy and Robert Giannini and Patricia Daley Giannini in Philadelphia were very kind to donate photographs.

Google and the Google logo are registered trademarks of Google Inc., used with permission. Magnum Photos, New York, granted permission as follows: Robert Capa (© International Center of Photography/Magnum Photos). Permission was obtained from the Bundesarchiv in Koblenz for several Wehrmacht images from Normandy.

Veterans have agreed over the years to talk about Normandy. I thank them for what they did then and were willing to share later: John Cotter, Henry Ferri, Peter Munger and a British gentleman I knew only as Jack.

This book would quite simply not have been possible without the National Archives in College Park, Maryland. Many staff provided assistance but a few stood out and must be mentioned: Andrew Knight in Cartography, and Sharon Culley, Holly Reed and Kaitlyn Crain Enriquez in Still Pictures.

My wife Meg Bleecker Blades and daughter Emma Blades provided much encouragement and were even willing to undertake thankless proofreading tasks. They did not seem to mind my absence on research trips including one in France and Holland. As always, their love and support sustain me.

This book is dedicated to my parents Winnie and Al Blades. My mother remembered the war as a time when she worked at the local telephone switchboard and worried about her brother in the Navy. She always wanted me to inquire into the past and I hope these efforts would have pleased her. My father served in the Pacific with the 1906th Engineer Aviation Battalion in New Guinea, Leyte and Okinawa. Little mention was made of the 50th anniversary of the Second World War before the D-Day commemorations in 1994. As a consequence, my father felt what they did in the Pacific perhaps did not matter. It did, Dad.

Strafford, Pennsylvania
April 2018

\*   \*   \*

Permission to publish excerpts was kindly granted by the following:

Excerpt from *Crusade in Europe* by Dwight D. Eisenhower, © 1948 by Doubleday, a division of Random House LLC. Used by permission of Doubleday, an imprint of the Knopf Doubleday Publishing Group, a division of Penguin Random House LLC. All rights reserved.

Matthew Daley interview, Oral History Collection, Special Collections & Archives, Florida State University Libraries, Tallahassee, Florida.

Cole Kingseed, *From Omaha Beach to Dawson's Ridge: The Combat Journal of Captain Joe Dawson*, © Naval Institute Press, Annapolis, Maryland.

Ed Wright letters in Wendell Wilkie Papers, Courtesy Lilly Library, Indiana University, Bloomington, Indiana.

# Introduction

What is the enduring appeal of Normandy in the study of the Second World War? D-Day and the Normandy campaign possess significance beyond the obvious beginning of the end for Nazi Germany. The late John Keegan recognized that military behaviours cannot be comprehended without reference to the broader cultural contexts that give rise to them. He understood the limitations in military history and the contributions made by S.L.A. Marshall in improving those historical narratives. Interviews conducted in Normandy both led to and in turn reinforced interpretations reflected in Marshall's later writings.[1]

Omaha Beach and other Normandy locations are sacred places to many today. The D-Day beaches were in large measure the primary gateways, the low doors in the Atlantic Wall that led, through heroism, suffering and sacrifice, to the liberation of Western Europe. To modern eyes, the landscapes associated with those events are memorialized and even sanitized to a point where the reality of those awful days in the summer of 1944 is increasingly hard to visualize. Even more regrettably, the people who occupied those landscapes and experienced those days have largely faded in person and public memory.

This volume proposes to revitalize both landscape and person, at least for the Americans who were there and the civilians they encountered. The intent is to reduce the immense scope of the invasion of France to a human scale that is both understandable and moving for the reader. The photographs presented herein include both famous and virtually unknown images.

The photographers also include those both legendary and obscure. Most were assigned to the Army Signal Corps who accompanied the infantry ashore. Many of these were commanded by Captain Herman Wall who himself landed on D-Day. Others were Naval or Coast Guard personnel or flew in Army Air Corps planes above the beaches. Robert Sargent recorded a remarkable series that included the most well-known American image of D-Day and one of the most famous photographs of the Second World War. Press photographers were also present both on the beaches and the interior of Normandy. Surely the most memorable was Robert Capa, who landed with the first wave of infantry on the eastern end of Omaha Beach. The photographs range from those posed for public relations benefit to some of the most candid images from the campaign.

This book is not dedicated to those photographers – richly deserving though they may be – but to their subjects and locations. Some of the images are reinterpreted or correctly identified as to location or subject for the first time. However, it is hoped that the reader will come to regard this volume as more than a collection of photographs, since the intent is to view them as interpretive documents to enhance a broader understanding of the 'soldiers, sailors and airmen' and others in Normandy.

The final D-Day plan that evolved over months of planning focused on Normandy, not on the Pas de Calais as the Germans were encouraged to expect. The number of divisions to be landed was increased from three to six, with an additional three airborne divisions to be landed at opposite ends of the invasion area. Due to rapid and variable tidal changes, the landings began earlier at the western end. The intent was to land early in the morning roughly one hour after low tide to enable invasion craft to avoid obstacles placed along the beaches. Such obstacles were designed to rip holes in the bottoms of landing craft or damage them through explosions of attached mines. All beaches were defended by guns in concrete emplacements, often designed to fire laterally along the beaches rather than out to sea. Such guns in *Widerstandsnest* (literally resistance nest) or strongpoint positions along the beach-front were supported by mortars and machine guns.

The D-Day assault beaches reflected a range of experiences. The 4th Division at Utah Beach on the Cotentin Peninsula sustained fewer casualties on 6 June than in earlier landing exercises off Slapton Sands in Devon, where nearly 1,000 soldiers were lost during an attack by German torpedo boats. The British and Canadian beach landings, while hardly unopposed, benefited from comparatively rapid movement inland although nothing like what had been hoped for. The landing of two American divisions on Omaha Beach was altogether different.

Critics of the American D-Day plan emerged early and have not ceased to this day. After the war Chester Wilmot was scathing in his criticism of the tactical operation plan for Omaha Beach. He decried a fundamental feature: the decision to assault the natural exits that were of course heavily defended. The troops that landed on less heavily defended beach sectors such as Dog White (or certain portions of Easy Red) fared much better.

The lack of interest by Omar Bradley and his staff in most of the 'funnies' designed by General Percy Hobart of the 79th Armoured Division was another point of criticism. Such heavy vehicles as 'Crab' flail tanks, flame-throwing tanks, and armoured vehicles for use by engineers were, according to Hobart, not requested by the Americans. Ironically, the items they did select – Duplex Drive or 'DD' tanks launched offshore as self-propelled floating vehicles – were abject failures in the rough seas. Wilmot argued that one of the hard-won lessons from Dieppe in 1942 was the need for combat engineers to have some form of armoured protection while attempting to clear beach obstacles.[2]

Criticisms of the tactical plan that were offered *prior* to the assault are even more telling. One of the most interesting sources of criticism was Brigadier General

Norman Cota, the assistant commander of the 29th Division, who landed on the western portion of Omaha Beach on D-Day morning. He had considerable experience with amphibious planning and argued for the creation of an 'Assault Division' that would land at night rather than at dawn. Lieutenant Jack Shea outlined the basic predictions that underlay Cota's argument for a landing during darkness, predictions that Shea contended were proven to be accurate:

- Naval fire will not be able to see targets well enough even during the day.
- Aerial bombardment will not eliminate all enemy positions.
- Landing errors will be made even in daylight.
- Daylight would do little more than provide better targets for defenders.
- The enemy would not be psychologically prepared to defend at night.

His proposal was characteristically bold but to no avail. Navy and Air Corps planners rejected the concept of a night assault.[3]

The landings by air and sea have received a tremendous amount of attention but they were only the beginning of the campaign. Bernard Montgomery emphasized that the battle for the beachheads in Normandy that commenced on D-Day would be the ultimate test of the cross-Channel strategy.[4] He commanded both British/Canadian and American forces during the first two months of the campaign. The general outline of his plan called for a steady buildup of Allied forces to permit an expansion of the beachhead. He expected that the Germans would concentrate their armoured forces near Caen and the eastern British/Canadian beaches to block the most direct route inland to Paris and the interior of France. It was intended that the Americans would expand westwards into the Cotentin Peninsula to capture Cherbourg and its port. The plan then called for movement southwards with the intent of breaking out of Normandy into Brittany to secure more ports needed to supply the ever increasing numbers of Allied soldiers in France.

Dwight Eisenhower, the supreme commander of the Allied Expeditionary Force, expected Montgomery to be more aggressive on his front while urging Bradley to establish early physical contact between the Omaha and Utah beachheads. Control of the town of Carentan therefore assumed considerable importance at the outset. Allied commanders were surprised that the German high command continued to expect another and perhaps larger invasion at the Pas de Calais but were dismayed by the stubborn resistance offered by enemy forces already in Normandy or hurriedly sent to the battle front.

The Norman *bocage* was composed of small fields enclosed by hedges and earthen embankments built up over centuries of plowing and farming. Such a landscape was ideal country for defence, particularly by German armour and infantry with anti-tank units. Caen to the east and Saint-Lô near the American forces were finally captured in July after tremendous fighting and much destruction. The stage was set for attempts to break through the thinning German lines on these respective fronts by late July. Allied air dominance played a crucial, perhaps decisive role throughout the campaign.

As mentioned above, the photographs in this book are intended to document the reality of the landscapes and the persons who lived and fought in them during the summer of 1944. The presentation is not linear and temporal but rather focuses on specific topics. The experiences of soldiers who arrived by air and sea and who fought through the *bocage* are illustrated, as are the German soldiers who opposed them and the French civilians who populated the landscape. Photographs documenting the treatment of American wounded and burial of American dead are presented, but it must not be forgotten that the advance and retreat of the armies could be measured in Norman villages destroyed and residents killed. Casualties among Allied and German forces were of course staggering.

Finally, this book is not dedicated solely to the past. The presentation will discuss surviving landscapes to provide a firm foundation for something modern scholars like to call 'memory'. Contemporary and future societies will redefine the memory of Omaha Beach and Normandy to suit their own ends. It is sincerely hoped this book will contribute to the larger effort of providing a material anchor for memory that will become increasingly important as the living memories of participants fade from the scene. Lastly, commemoration and efforts to counter the manipulation of memory are fundamental components in the promotion of what the British scholar Paul Richards termed 'a just and lasting peace'.

# Chapter One

# **Preparations in England**

Winston Churchill experienced his best night's sleep since the beginning of the war after he learned of the Japanese attack on Pearl Harbor in December 1941. The United States would then inevitably be drawn into the war in Europe and against Japan. Any uncertainty vanished when Hitler declared war on America a few days later. Churchill realized the entry of her massive manpower and industrial would assure victory.

The power of the American economy even following an era of economic depression was astounding. A former automotive factory could produce a single bomber aircraft in approximately an hour. Arsenals manufactured millions of cartridges each day. Shipyards on both coasts built the naval warships and cargo vessels required to transport men and equipment across oceans. All of this industrial capacity lay beyond the reach of enemy air forces and thus could proceed undisturbed. U-boats did pose a threat but one increasingly countered by Allied use of escorted convoys and air patrols.

The Allies possessed another advantage of immense importance: they could read German wireless messages. The story of breaking the Enigma encryptions at Bletchley Park and the resulting flood of intelligence known by the code word Ultra emerged some thirty years after the end of the war. Ultra intelligence revealed the success of deception efforts regarding the location and timing of the invasion, the disposition of many Wehrmacht and Luftwaffe units and the increasing limitations of fuel and transport resulting from repeated attacks by Allied air forces. German use of telephones for communication resulted in gaps in Ultra data, but wireless transmissions yielded a wealth of information on divisional strength, defensive dispositions and tactical plans for counter-attacks following the fall of Carentan in June and near Mortain in early August.[5] Ultra would save countless lives but the authorities who controlled that intelligence knew the cost in lives in the upcoming invasion would still be considerable.

American naval and air forces had been building up in England since 1942 and both had engaged German targets in the Atlantic and in the skies over Europe. Nevertheless, it was recognized that the liberation of France and Western Europe would require massive quantities of infantry and armoured units. Soldiers from many

European nations had begun to assemble in Britain since 1940. The American and British general staffs disagreed on strategic priorities and on when to invade. Eventually it was decided to direct the first major American effort in late 1942 to Morocco, Algeria and Tunisia to assist British soldiers driving westwards along the Mediterranean coast. In 1943 the Allied forces would invade Sicily and then attack the Italian mainland. American troops that had battle experience before the invasion of Normandy had gained that experience in the Mediterranean theatre.

American army units began to arrive in Britain in 1942, including the three infantry regiments in the 29th Division. Two lieutenants in the 116th Infantry – Matthew Daley and Ernest Wise – were among these early arrivals, stationed at Bristowe. The 90th Division that would land as a reserve unit on Utah Beach was posted in the west of England; Private John Cotter, an archaeologist who was older than many in his outfit, would accompany that division. Private Henri Ferri would arrive in France on D-Day with a military police company attached to the 37th Engineer Combat Battalion.

In early 1944, the 299th Engineer Combat Battalion was training in the southern United States. Most of that battalion – including Captain Matthew Perry and Company A – would land on Omaha Beach. So would the 1st Division that had fought in North Africa and Sicily, although its veteran regiments would include numbers of young replacements by early 1944.

The young American soldiers who arrived in England encountered a strange world that seemed similar in terms of language but only just so. Consumption of warm beer and navigating vehicles on the opposite – to them the wrong – side of roads reinforced the alien nature of the land they had 'invaded' in preparation for their landings in Europe. Some soldiers, particularly draftees, wondered why they were there to fight in a 'European' war. They were engaged in what Paul Fussell termed 'the Boys' Crusade' because of their youth.[6] One such youth was Peter Munger who graduated from Lower Merion High School in suburban Philadelphia in June 1944. By the end of the summer he was assigned to the 30th Division in Normandy and narrowly missed being caught up in the deadly advance to Saint-Lô and the German counter-offensive near Mortain.

Youth was certainly prevalent among the divisions the Americans were assembling for the invasion but this was not exclusively the case. Edward Wright from Brooklyn entered the army in 1943 and was trained as an infantryman. He was in his thirties and older than many of his fellow trainees. He had participated in New York political affairs and maintained an extensive correspondence with prominent persons including Wendell Wilkie, the Republican nominee for president in 1940. Wright combined the articulate writing of a college graduate with the informed perspectives of an enlisted man to describe his training battalion in late 1943 as 'largely youngsters of 18 or 19, and family men over 30'.[7] He subsequently expanded his description to focus on morale and the seeming unreality of military training:

> Basic is tough, especially on the older men, though in some respects I think it is not tough enough for preparation for combat. There is something unrealistic about simulating the operation of weapons, about night problems led by acting squad leaders who are neither soldiers nor woodsmen in any real sense, and about other phases of the program.
>
> For the most part, the men I know here are not yet at war emotionally or in spirit. In some respects we are an Army of remnants, older men and men who would have been rejected earlier for physical reasons. The spirit does not seem quite the same as it did with the earlier part of the Army, composed chiefly of our best youngsters.
>
> Few of us can really believe that we are really training to fight and kill, that we will ever be part of a genuine skirmish line ... I think most men here confidently expect the Russians to be in Warsaw and Belgrade within a matter of weeks, followed by a swift German collapse, which will in turn make the war with Japan a swift march. Whether there is any real justification for this feeling, I don't know, but it does not help to turn us into eager soldiers. Though the first shock of combat will undoubtedly do so.[8]

Within two months Wright was sent to the Mediterranean where he would be assigned as part of the replacements to the 88th Division in Italy. Serving at least initially with strangers rather than friends made during training, he would march into Rome on the night of 3/4 June just before D-Day in France.

The American airborne units were certain they would be drawn into combat in some theatre. One of the best reflections of the challenges related to invasion preparations is provided in the diary of Brigadier General James Gavin, assistant commander of the 82nd Airborne Division. He described problems with command in several units, including the veteran 505th Parachute Infantry that had landed in Sicily. He doubted whether officers in other regiments in the division would be effective leaders in combat. Subsequently some were killed or captured while others proved to be highly effective. He emphasized defence against armour and more generally that training was 'the time to drive home the proper techniques'. Gavin believed 'the decisive A/B battle is fought on the ground of the A/B commander's selection, there are no retrograde movements.'[9]

Gavin commented on the rigours of camp life for the enlisted men and decried the tendency of officers to obtain better housing for themselves. Winter exercises were unpleasant but necessary, as would be understood later in the Ardennes. During jump training one soldier in the 507th Parachute Infantry placed a wooden paddle in the pack perhaps to 'tuck in flaps' during deployment. The main chute only opened about one-quarter of its full extent, the reserve chute became entangled in the main and he was killed in the fall.[10]

There were also social problems to be addressed. In late February problems erupted with local African American units who had been in the Leicester area for a longer period of time and became friends with many local civilians. Gavin noted that following the arrival of white American troops 'frays and minor unpleasant encounters have occurred in the local pubs and dance halls. American whites resent very much seeing a white woman in the company of a colored soldier.' One night a group of African American soldiers had armed themselves and were driving a truck into town. One of their officers convinced them to return to camp and thus not confront officers from the 505th who were themselves armed.[11]

No doubt officers in command and particularly those charged with keeping the peace would be relieved when the invasion orders were finally received. The landings scheduled for 5 June were postponed by one day due to weather. Gavin's diary entry on the day before D-Day expressed his simultaneous feelings of anxiety and confidence: 'Visited all fields this morning. Troops are in top condition and morale couldn't be higher. They are ready anxious and confident … I expect this to be my hardest fight and I hope my last with unseasoned troops such as the 08 and 07 [508th and 507th Parachute Infantry Regiments]. They will do well as is becoming American parachutists.'[12]

Captain Chester Hansen, aide to Omar Bradley, had sailed from Bristol to Plymouth with the staff of First Army a few days earlier:

> Soon the water boiled with minesweepers and small escort craft. The British Naval ensign was everywhere in the wind. The enormous letters and numbers of the LCTs stood out bravely on their sides. A rocket craft passed us with her bank of deadly rockets in place for the invasion. Her crew was checking the guns, writing letters, reading books. This was the invasion. This is what we waited for through three years of war. The ships carry a grim, throbbing atmosphere about them, but there were no demonstrations, no cheering. We were sailing off to the continent, but no one seemed unduly excited about the prospect.[13]

Within a few days the largest invasion fleet ever assembled sailed from ports all along the southern coast of England for Normandy.

A practice jump by the 506th Parachute Infantry Regiment of the 101st Airborne Division near Newbury, England, photographed by Runyan on 16 November 1943. He would accompany the division to Normandy. *(NARA)*

Second Lieutenant Matthew Daley from Company F, 116th Infantry, in camp at Bristowe, 2 February 1944.

*(Robert Giannini and Patricia Daley Giannini)*

(**Above left**) First Lieutenant Ernest Wise, F/116th executive officer in Bristowe in late 1943 or early 1944. (*Robert Giannini and Patricia Daley Giannini*)

(**Above right**) Officers of Company A, 299th Engineer Combat Battalion in late 1943 or early 1944 before shipping out for England. From left to right, Lieutenants Apt, Elmer Donahoo, Ed Perry (later captain) and Jack Wood. Lieutenants Donahoo and Wood would be wounded on Omaha Beach on D-Day. (*Michael Perry*)

(**Right**) From left to right, First Sergeant Norman Laugel and Staff Sergeants Harold Stilwell and Emil Chabuel from A/299th. After D-Day Captain Perry marked Stilwell as missing and the others as not present. (*Michael Perry*)

An infantry unit poses on 1 April 1944. *(NARA)*

LCI 93 (landing craft infantry) and LCT 489 (landing craft tank) assault a practice beach in southern England in May 1944. Tanks, other vehicles and infantry are present. *(NARA)*

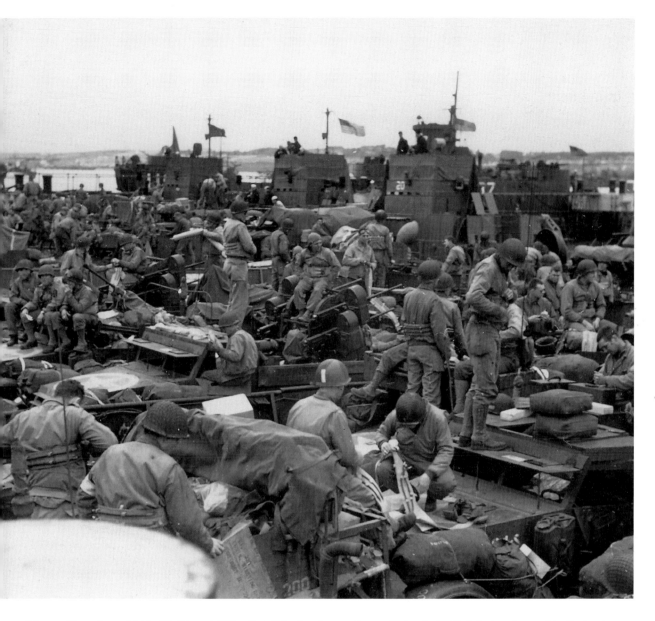

(**Opposite, above**) LCIs 87, 84 and 497 with LCAs (landing craft assault) loaded with infantry at a port in England early in June. The LCI vessels were destined for Omaha Beach. (*NARA*)

(**Opposite, below**) Troops of the 1st Division and armoured forces possibly from the 741st Tank Battalion pose for the camera in southern England. (*NARA*)

(**Above**) Soldiers examining equipment and putting on life belts amid a mass of half-tracks and amphibious vessels poised for the invasion. (*NARA*)

(**Opposite, above**) A company-sized infantry unit march to an embarkation area in early June. The sign on the background wall is marked Cornwall, suggesting the infantry may have been from the 29th Division. (*NARA*)

(**Opposite, below**) Troops loading onto LCIs. (*NARA*)

(**Above**) An LCT (possibly No. 821) in Dartmouth with self-propelled artillery already loaded on 1 June. (*NARA*)

(**Left**) Members of the 2nd Ranger Battalion await the invasion in Weymouth on 1 June. The second soldier in the rear row without a helmet – Sergeant Walter Geldon from Company C – would not survive the landing on Omaha Beach. (*NARA*)

Nehez photographed the loading of an LCVP (landing craft vehicles and troops) and thirty-six men in Torquay on 3 June. (*NARA*)

# Chapter Two

# Airborne Landings on the Cotentin Peninsula

The airborne operations in Operation Neptune or the actual Normandy invasion were the largest undertaken to that point in the Second World War and therefore in the history of warfare. As a consequence, they were controversial at the time. The scope of the American operations on the Cotentin Peninsula was sharply criticized by Air Chief Marshal Trafford Leigh-Mallory, who was himself a controversial figure for his opposition to Hugh Dowding's leadership of Fighter Command during the Battle of Britain; Leigh-Mallory thought the airborne effort should be scaled back or even cancelled. When Omar Bradley stated he would not undertake the landings at Utah Beach without airborne troops inland to secure the exits, Leigh-Mallory insisted that Bradley bear any consequences for the outcome. The latter responded he was accustomed to accepting responsibility for operations under his command.[14]

The route to the final airborne plan was by no means straightforward. Various proposals were offered, including landings well inland between the Rivers Seine and Loire that would surely have been disastrous. During the winter of 1944 James Gavin heard rumours of a separate undertaking on the Brest Peninsula. He favoured the idea at the time, since he believed there was a general feeling the airborne plans 'lack vision and boldness' and were, in the words of one critic, 'like having Michelangelo paint a barn'. Gavin later began to wonder if the plans for Normandy were a ruse. Rather than making an effort where the enemy was strongest – fifty-six divisions were thought to be present in France – he came to believe 'The Balkans is the place, I would not be a bit surprised if we went there.'[15]

The plan to drop the 82nd Airborne near Saint-Sauveur-le-Vicomte to assist in cutting off the Cotentin Peninsula at its base was abandoned late in May when evidence of additional defensive measures appeared. The division was eventually dropped astride the Merderet River with the intention of securing the inland flank of the Utah landings and the important road junction of Sainte-Mère-Église. The mission of the 101st Airborne Division was consequently modified to allow a greater concentration near the coast behind Utah Beach.

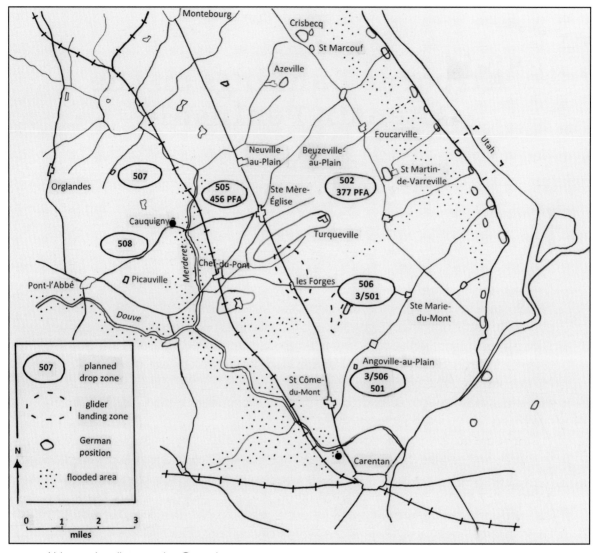

Airborne Landings on the Cotentin. (*After Ruppenthal,* Utah Beach to Cherbourg)

The theatre historical officer Colonel S.L.A. Marshall devoted a considerable amount of personal research during the summer of 1944 to documenting and understanding those operations. (The use of Marshall's research in this work is confined to the early manuscript reports derived from certain group and individual interviews he conducted in Normandy.) There were several reasons for this intense interest. Marshall was aware of the exceptional nature of these efforts, including large-scale use of gliders and the fragility of lightly-armed airborne troops once they had landed. He was fascinated by airborne operations, and contrasted them with the experiences of traditional infantry: 'The ordinary foot soldier today knows that if he receives a serious wound he still has a good chance to recover, because of plasma and the other wonders of modern medicine. The airborne soldier must realize that in the same circumstances he will probably die because the chances are that the supply will not be there or the conditions will be such that his comrades will have to move on and leave him to his own resources. One finds in this record many examples of heroic effort by medical men and by other parachutists on behalf of their wounded. But one must note also the numerous occasions when the wounded have to be disregarded or when they suffer and then die because adequate relief cannot be had. This must be one of the main considerations weighing on the morale of airborne troops.'[16]

Marshall also drew attention to the complex 'psychological change and shock' associated with airborne landings as opposed to traditional land combat. He argued conventional infantry would experience 'only one sustained wave of apprehension' before combat; those troops that landed by sea on D-Day would probably have disputed this particular assertion. The anxieties associated with airborne transport and entry into battle were, according to Marshall, multiple and complex in nature:[17]

- Anxiety and fear of jump, followed by stimulation of actual drop brought on by adrenalin and subsequent fatigue; Marshall cited prevailing wisdom that the effort associated with an airborne jump was as exhausting as a full work day.[18]
- Once a paratrooper descends he is either engaged in combat or lands unopposed and is elated to have survived.
- The soldier may again become depressed upon finding himself alone in enemy country. Many became immobile and sought shelter despite their training. Gavin stated this was particularly true among those 82nd soldiers unfamiliar with combat. Since Normandy was the introduction to combat for the entire 101st Airborne, only one parachute regiment of the six in both divisions – the 505th in the 82nd – had previously engaged enemy forces.
- When daylight appears, confidence begins to rise as troops have often managed to assemble in small groups. A sense of accomplishment at having survived emerges as the darkness disappears. However, such confidence was both illusory and dangerous. Leaders must begin to push tired and disorientated soldiers toward their appointed missions.
- Once the enemy is engaged, the paratroopers finally experience the reaction to combat common to any infantry.

Marshall indicated that an active debate was ongoing concerning tactics in the immediate aftermath of a parachute drop. Junior officers seemed to prefer moving forward in small groups as soon as such groups were assembled. More senior officers emphasized the importance of gathering larger company or battalion units to undertake more difficult and important missions. Whatever the respective merits, opinions were derived from the command perspectives of the two groups. While it was clearly desirable to gather groups that were as large as possible, it was equally clear to Marshall that small accumulations under the leadership of dedicated officers or forceful personalities accomplished great things on D-Day.

The photographs of airborne soldiers reflect the mixture and blending of units from the two divisions that was common in the night-time drop into Normandy. The dispersion of troops across the Cotentin proved to be something of a virtue since it resulted in great confusion among the German defenders. Marshall noted in numerous interviews a consistent enemy tendency to stoutly defend positions but not to take assertive offensive action.

Combat conditions were rarely shown in the airborne photographs. Views of these soldiers appear throughout the volume, including a patrol northwards to the village of Saint-Marcouf. The most frequent scenes are those of paratroopers with civilians or holding positions in and near towns. Efforts to defend or capture towns at strategic locations such as the 82nd Airborne at Sainte-Mère-Église and the Merderet River and the 101st Airborne at Carentan reveal some of the challenges faced by paratroopers during their first week in Normandy.

## The Merderet Causeway

The 505th Parachute Infantry had the most successful drop early on D-Day, with much of the regiment landing on their zone north-west of Sainte-Mère-Église. The 3rd Battalion proceeded to enter and capture the town, raising the same flag they had used in Naples earlier in the war. The 2nd Battalion also entered to assist their sister battalion in the defence of roadblocks at this important crossroads town. Before that, however, their commander Lieutenant Colonel Benjamin Vandervoort had sent a reinforced platoon from Company D under Lieutenant Turner Turnbull to block the road at Neuville-au-Plain, the northern approach to Sainte-Mère-Église. Their defence lasted for hours, by which time only sixteen of the roughly forty-two paratroopers were able to withdraw southwards.[19] However, they had protected the northern access to the town as its defenders were occupied with attacks from the south. Marshall considered the decision by Vandervoort and the consequent action by Turnbull to be among the most important taken by the airborne on D-Day, an opinion later reflected by James Gavin and John Keegan.

The 1st Battalion had an altogether different experience west of the town at the bridge and causeway across the flooded Merderet River. Company A attempted to seize the bridge through direct assault but was stymied by a small group of stubborn defenders in stone buildings near La Fière at the eastern end. Numerous casualties were sustained; among those shot dead were the commander and deputy commander of the battalion. Company G from the 507th Parachute Infantry under Captain Floyd Schwartzwalder discovered a sideroad parallel to the flooded fields

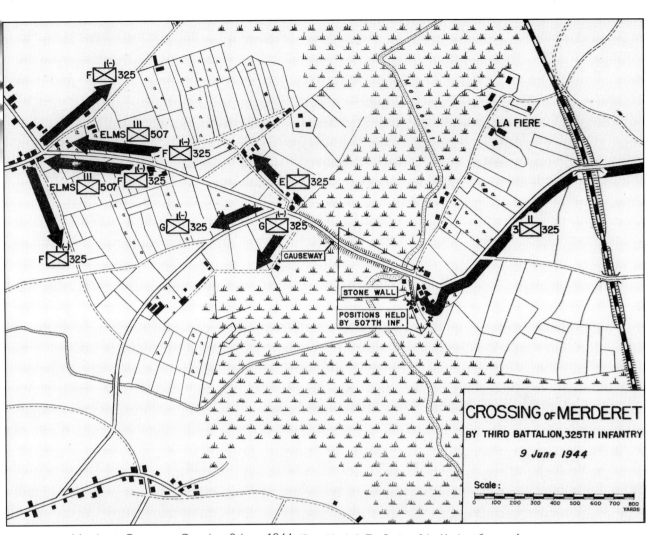

Merderet Causeway Crossing, 9 June 1944. (*From Marshall, 'The Forcing of the Merderet Causeway'*)

that enabled them to cross the bridge and causeway to the west side. There they encountered a small group of Americans who had landed on the west side. Had they been able to hold the position, a major goal of the 82nd Airborne would have been accomplished.

However, the 507th group moved northwards to join other elements of their regiment and became isolated with them for several days. German counter-attacks drove the remaining American defenders – including a company from the 508th that had just crossed – from the western end of the causeway and even approached the eastern bank, although the bridgehead at that end held. Marshall pointed out that the failure to secure the western end on D-Day presented the division with a problem that would dominate its efforts for days and cost hundreds of casualties.[20]

The 325th Glider Infantry landed on 7 June. Numerous casualties were incurred due to glider crashes that were thought to have resulted from their release at roughly

200 feet, making it difficult for the pilots to land in the small fields.[21] The 1/325th was sent across the Merderet on a sunken roadway north of the causeway on 8 June but was compelled to retreat by a strong German counter-attack. Private Charles DeGlopper fired a BAR (Browning automatic rifle) from an exposed position until being killed by enemy fire. His actions enabled many of his comrades to withdraw, for which DeGlopper was awarded the Medal of Honor.[22]

By 9 June (D+3) the divisional commander Matthew Ridgway insisted a bridgehead be opened on the west bank. The 3/325th was selected to make the assault. An artillery preparation was called upon but little to no smoke was laid down to conceal the infantry. The glider troops had to advance down an open causeway against pre-pared positions. Casualties were of course expected but the troops were encour-aged to keep moving forward rather than seeking the scant shelter afforded along the causeway. When troops did stop, they created bottlenecks that impeded the advance of others trying to move forward.

Once on the west side Company G peeled off to the south, while Company E moved past the Cauquigny church to the north. Company F advanced straight forward towards high ground at Le Motey. A group of 507th paratroopers under the command of Captain Robert Rae had been held in reserve by Gavin and was sent forward when the assault appeared to falter, a situation that the 3/325th later con-tended did not occur. The advance into Le Motey carried so far forward that it was blunted both by German resistance and American artillery fire from the east bank. Casualties were later placed at 40 killed and 180 wounded[23] and were heaviest among those who had halted on the causeway. By evening a bridgehead of troops from various units had been established and included the soldiers from the 507th who had been isolated in an orchard since D-Day.

## The Carentan Causeway

The 101st Airborne was charged with the task of securing the southern flank of the airborne bridgehead and establishing a linkage with the infantry advancing westwards from the Omaha Beach landings. The town of Carentan was a pivotal point in that linkage.

The 3rd Battalion of the 502nd Parachute Infantry was selected to make the advance on the western edge of Carentan on 11 June. To achieve this goal, they had to advance along a causeway and cross four bridges, the second of which had been largely destroyed and the fourth (and final) one mostly blocked by an iron gate.

The challenge facing Lieutenant Colonel Robert Cole and the companies of the 3/502nd was to maintain the initiative of advance once they had crossed the last bridge to positions on the south bank of the Madeleine River and marshes near Carentan. He therefore decided upon an unusual approach: a bayonet charge upon the German trenches. He informed his second-in-command Major John Stopka to

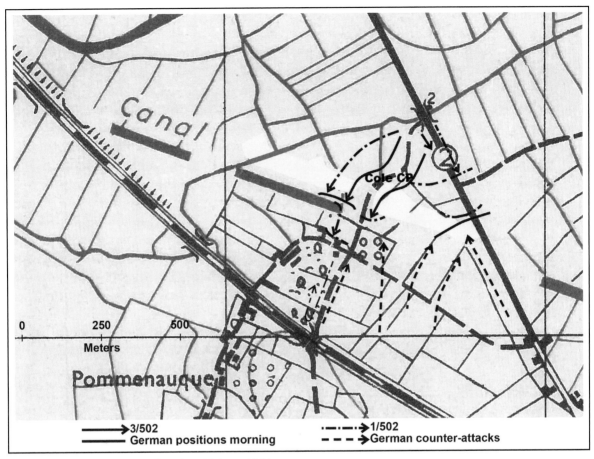

Carentan Causeway Crossing, 11 June 1944.

pass along instructions to advance when he blew a whistle. Artillery smoke was called; Cole and men near him rose up, followed by Stopka and some more soldiers. Others joined the attack when they saw it beginning, while many never figured out what was happening. However, the numbers were sufficient to capture both the enemy trenches and a nearby farm house in which Cole established his command post. However, the difficulties were just beginning for the 3/502nd.

The battle was a strange one, with two out of three of the paratroopers stating they never saw the enemy at any point during the engagement, only later as casualties. Additional troops arrived from the 1/502nd to assist in holding the position, at one place occupying positions behind a stone wall while Germans held a vine-covered wall or hedgerow on the opposite side of a road. The Germans counter-attacked in the morning and again during the afternoon and the situation began to look bleak to Cole. Finally a radio link was established with American artillery. Supporting fire passed just over the farm house and landed so close to American positions that two injured paratroopers – Sergeant Charles DeRose and Lieutenant Frank Magrie – were killed. The German attack eased from that point onward.

When Marshall later asked Cole during the interview session why so few had joined in the charge, Cole responded, 'Colonel, they were afraid, that's why.' Marshall had difficulty accepting such a straightforward explanation and probed more deeply. What emerged was a confusion of orders in the military version of whisper-down-the-lane used to transmit them. Cole later expressed his appreciation for the clarification. The historical account was informed by a tour of the battlefield that occurred a scant two weeks after the engagement. One of the surprises to Marshall was the virtual absence of artillery impact holes in the fields and hedgerows despite the importance placed upon the 'very intense' barrage.

The value of unit interviews by Marshall conducted shortly after actions was never so obvious than in this instance. The importance of the accounts obtained by the History Section was sadly reinforced by the fact that neither Cole nor Stopka survived the war. Cole was killed in Best, Holland, on 18 September before learning he had been awarded the Medal of Honor for the Carentan action. Stopka was killed by 'friendly fire' at Bastogne in early January.[24]

(**Right**) A trooper from the 101st Airborne Division prepares to enplane for Normandy on the evening of 5 June. (*NARA*)

(**Opposite page**) A heavily laden paratrooper struggles to board a transport aircraft on the same evening. Both photographs were recorded by Nehez. (*NARA*)

ETO-HQ-44-4718

(**Above**) A 'stick' or plane load of 16 paratroopers from the 101st Airborne Division on board and possibly en route to Normandy. (*NARA*)

(**Opposite, above**) A plane load of 101st paratroopers waiting to board a C-47. Both photographs by Nehez on the evening of 5 June. (*NARA*)

(**Opposite, below**) A column of paratroopers probably from the 82nd Airborne Division marching to transport aircraft at Middle Wallop on the evening of 5 June, as photographed by Meyer. (*NARA*)

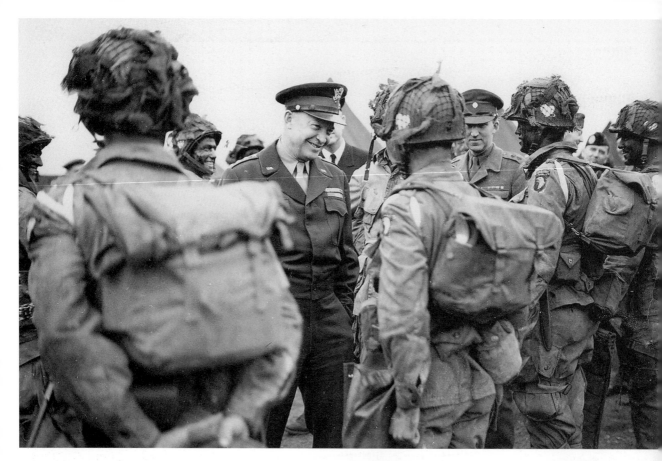

The photographer Moore recorded images of commanders during the Normandy campaign, including General Dwight Eisenhower addressing airborne soldiers on the evening of 5 June. John Keegan indicated the unit was Company E, 502nd Parachute Infantry. On 30 May, Air Marshal Leigh-Mallory had protested what he thought would be the 'futile slaughter' of two fine divisions. Eisenhower described the visit: 'A late evening trip on the fifth took me to the camp of the U.S. 101st Airborne Division, one of the units whose participation had been so severely questioned by the air commander. I found the men in fine fettle, many of them joshingly admonishing me that I had no cause for worry, since the 101st was on the job and everything would be taken care of in fine shape. I stayed with them until the last of them were in the air, somewhere about midnight' (Eisenhower, *Crusade in Europe*, pp. 251–2). *(NARA)*

Gliders landing at the crossroads on the high ground near Blosville with C-47 tow planes turning away overhead. Numerous vehicles including tracked armoured vehicles from the beach are visible on the highway N13 and around the cluster of houses at Les Forges. A small armoured force and the 3rd Battalion, 8th Infantry had come inland from Utah Beach to the area on the night of 6 June. The photo was probably taken on the morning of 7 June when the 8th Infantry (4th Division) assisted by the armoured force attacked northward towards Sainte-Mère-Église (Ruppenthal, *Utah Beach to Cherbourg*, pp. 53–4, 61–2) as units of the 325th Glider Infantry were landing. (*NARA*)

A modern photograph of the location showing the new highway. (*Google Earth*)

A portion of the 1944 AMS map with the superimposed locations of this aerial photograph (low-level oblique) and the two that follow as rectangles. (*NARA*)

Gliders among hedgerow-bordered fields north of the Blosville high ground. These aircraft probably transported the glider infantry to D+1 landings 'from the main highway running between Sainte-Mère-Église and Carentan eastward to the beach' (Marshall, 'Initial Operations of 325th Glider Infantry', p. 1 in 'Combat Interviews 82nd Airborne Division Operation Neptune'). Some gliders were damaged on landing; the dark circular patches were probably isolated trees. (NARA)

A modern view of the location reveals that a substantial number of the hedgerows remain intact. (Google Earth)

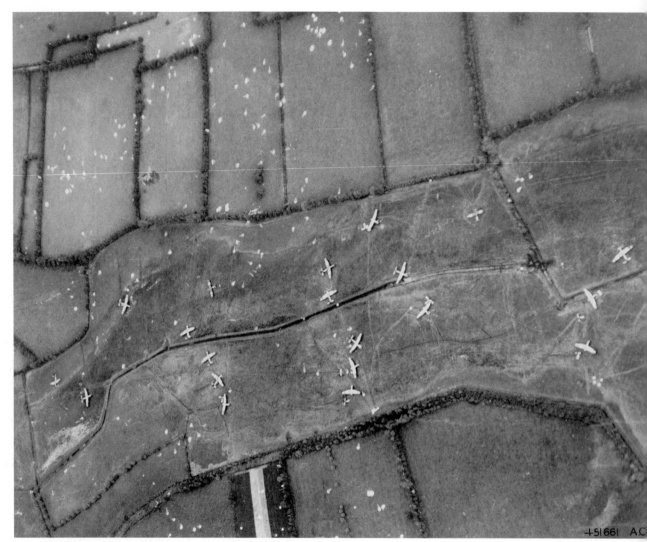

+51661 A C

(**Above**) A glider landing area south of Turqueville about 2km east of the area shown in the previous two images. In this instance, parachute infantry had already landed in the zone. The location was close to where some sticks (plane loads) of the 3rd Battalion 501st Parachute Infantry had landed early on D-Day (Ruppenthal, *Utah Beach to Cherbourg*, Map 4) between Drop Zones A and C. (*NARA*)

(**Opposite, above**) The modern view shows more extensive landscape modification. (*Google Earth*)

(**Opposite, below**) 82nd Airborne Division officers and guards in Sainte-Mère-Église on 6 June as photographed by Witscher. The taller officer has trousers wet to the knees due to flooded conditions in nearby areas. He may be Colonel William Ekman, commander of the 505th Parachute Infantry, or Lieutenant Colonel Edward Krause of the regiment's 3rd Battalion. The commander of the 1st Battalion, Major Frederick Kellam, was killed near the Merderet bridge that morning. Lieutenant Colonel Ben Vandervoort of the 2nd Battalion had broken his leg during the landing and was finding movement difficult. (*NARA*)

This glider had landed successfully and subsequently provided shade and shelter for some of the famous Norman dairy cows. Norbie recorded this image on 7 June probably on the landing fields near Blosville. (*NARA*)

A smoke-filled street in Sainte-Mère-Église on 8 June as photographed by Witscher. (*NARA*)

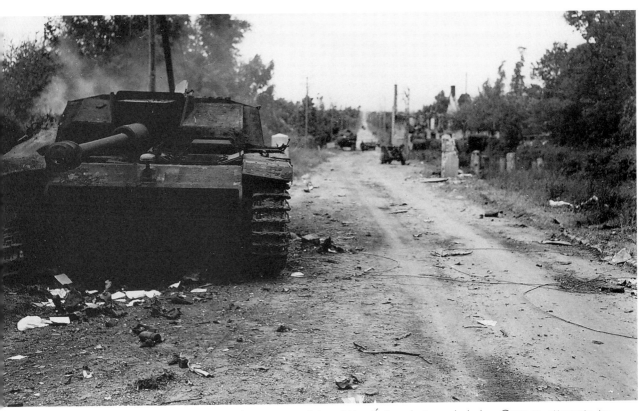

Smouldering *Sturmgeschütz* type III assault gun near Sainte-Mère-Église destroyed during German attempts to recapture the town as photographed by Franklin on 10 June. *(NARA)*

Soldiers of the 82nd Airborne on mounted patrol in Sainte-Mère-Église on 10 June as photographed by Franklin. *(NARA)*

(**Above**) Kaye photographed a rifle squad probably from the 501st Parachute Infantry, 101st Airborne Division standing with local residents in Sainte-Marie-du-Mont on 7 June. One of the young women offered a bottle of wine to the liberators. (*NARA*)

(**Opposite, above**) The structures are largely unchanged today.

(**Opposite, below**) A mixed group of airborne soldiers from the 82nd and 101st Divisions moving through Sainte-Marie-du-Mont, photographed by Kaye on 12 June. Confused and overlapping drops were typical in Normandy. (*NARA*)

View of causeway facing east towards Le Manoir at La Fière, possibly in June or summer 1944. *(Marshall Collection)*

Modern view of causeway facing east towards the stone buildings of Le Manoir.

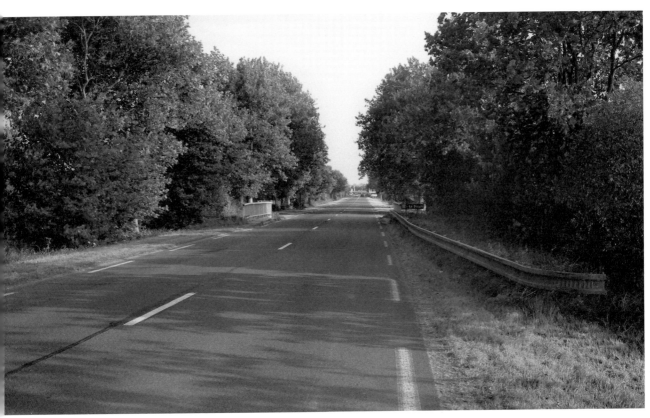

Modern view of causeway facing south from the third bridge to the Carentan area.

View of road behind Ingouf Farm showing the battlefield of 11 June, probably recorded in late June 1944 when Colonel Marshall toured the battlefield with Lieutenant Colonel Cole. *(Marshall Collection)*

(**Opposite, above**) Modern view of house on former Ingouf Farm used as headquarters by Lieutenant Colonel Cole and 3/502nd Parachute Infantry on 11 June 1944.

(**Above**) View of walls flanking road in Pommenauque, south of Ingouf Farm. During the afternoon of 11 June the 1/502nd held the stone wall at right while Germans were positioned behind the vine-covered wall on the left side of the road. The photograph was probably recorded in late June 1944. (*Marshall Collection*)

(**Opposite, below**) Paratroopers of the 101st Airborne pass casualties – the caption suggested due to snipers – in the vicinity of Carentan on 14 June. The photograph may have been staged since such an advance was not prudent if snipers were present. (*NARA*)

101st medics inspect a destroyed house in Carentan on 14 June (Collier). *(NARA)*

Army photographer Runyan entered Carentan with the 101st and recorded numerous images during the first days in the town including the following ones. He photographed a fire on a street near a medical column on 12 June. (*NARA*)

A medical column moves through Carentan, probably on 14 June following the capture of the town on 12 June. American jeeps and a German truck are shown. (*NARA*)

(**Opposite, above**) A jeep with a vertical bar for cutting wires strung across roads passed civilians in Carentan on the same day. (*NARA*)

(**Opposite, below**) Soldiers from the 101st Airborne move through Carentan in a captured German *Kübelwagen* on 14 June. The presence of the 327th Glider Infantry is indicated by the club-shaped stencil on the helmet of a soldier along the house wall. That regiment continued the assault on Carentan following the causeway crossing by the 502nd. (*NARA*)

(**Above**) Rubble and burning houses in Carentan on 17 June. The Germans wanted to re-establish their defense of the town. (*NARA*)

German artillery fire falls near a bridge in Carentan. The bridges across the River Douve enabled the forces from Utah and Omaha to establish a unified beachhead. (NARA)

# Chapter Three

# Landings on Easy Red and Fox Green

The 16th Infantry of the 1st Division crossed the English Channel in assault transports on the night of 5 June. The 1st Battalion (1/16th) boarded the *Samuel Chase*, which also carried photographers Robert Capa and Robert Sargent. Capa aboard the *Chase* described a breakfast of pancakes, sausages, eggs and coffee largely ignored by the preoccupied soldiers.[25]

The 2nd Battalion (2/16th) was carried aboard the *Henrico*. Reveille sounded at 0100 on 6 June. Breakfast was served commencing at 0130, consisting of black coffee and sandwiches of bologna and luncheon meat regarded as 'not very appetizing'. The soldiers were called to their LCVP (landing craft vehicles and personnel) and loaded between 0330 and 0400. The boats were lowered, assembled and began heading towards shore shortly before 0500. Companies E and F, each between 180 and 190 men, were included in the first wave. Company G was intended to land shortly afterwards.

The troops viewed seaborne transport with feelings of ambivalence. Confined to cramped assault craft such as LCVP that were open to the wind and the sea, most soldiers were soaked as they approached the beaches. Those who had attempted to consume breakfast often regretted the decision since sea sickness was common. On occasions craft were swamped or struck by mines or artillery, thus eliminating entire sections of thirty or so men as effective combat units. The larger LCI (landing craft infantry) with nearly 200 men aboard represented still greater losses when damaged.

As the boats moved closer to shore, they passed men floating in the water. Their initial thought was that these were downed airmen but they proved to be survivors of Duplex Drive (DD) tanks that had sunk in the rough seas. The line of departure was about 2,000 yards from the beach; Company G reached this point about 0630. By that time, the earliest waves were threading through numerous obstacles and the boats were lowering ramps. The invasion of France had begun for the 1st Division.

Many in the 1st Division thought they should never have been selected to participate in Operation Neptune. The division, known as 'The Big One' due to its shoulder

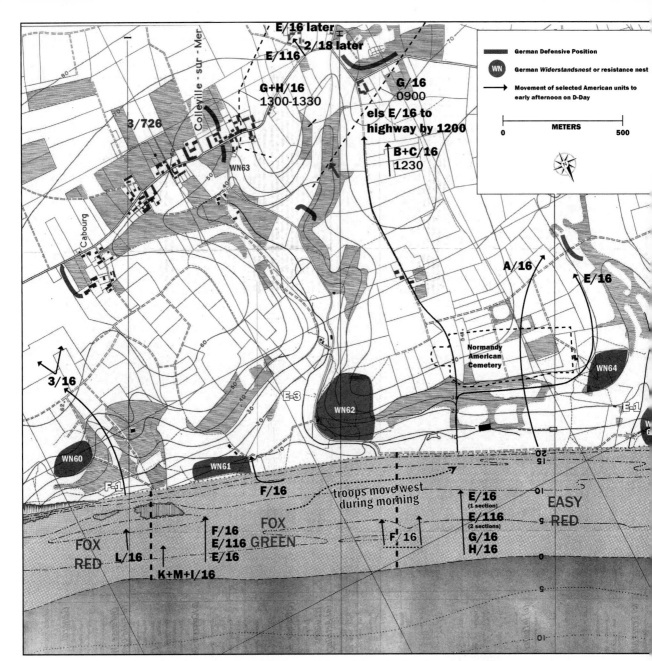

Early Landings on and Advance from Eastern End of Omaha Beach.

patch or 'The Fighting First'[26] based on its legendary reputation, had participated in two amphibious landings before Normandy. The regiments in the division had individually or collectively been humbled at Kasserine and redeemed at El Guettar and near Hill 609 in Tunisia. They had invaded Sicily and fought across the island to Troina. Those veterans who survived by the end of 1943 believed their performance to date entitled the division to be sent home.

The division's leadership – Generals Terry Allen and Theodore Roosevelt, Jr., as commander and assistant commander respectively – was equally legendary. Fiercely proud of the division, they fostered a culture of independence and superiority that became troubling to army leadership, particularly Omar Bradley. Roosevelt – cousin and fierce critic of President Franklin Roosevelt – had supposedly informed his soldiers that only officers from the 1st Division should be saluted. Bradley later stated that he had decided at the beginning of the campaign for Sicily to relieve Allen and as a consequence Roosevelt. Although various reasons were given, he ultimately concluded that both 'had sinned by loving the division too much'. Allen left for the United States only to return to Europe in command of the 104th Division. Roosevelt landed on Utah Beach on D-Day as assistant commander of the 4th Division.

Bradley placed Clarence Huebner in command of the veteran division. His task was not an enviable one. Many officers felt the removal of the divisional commander was completely unjustified and undoubtedly blamed Bradley and others. However, Huebner had been commissioned during the First World War, knew the 1st Division well and was a disciplinarian. Huebner evidently thought the division needed the same adjustment in attitude that George Patton brought to the North African theatre. By the time of the Normandy invasion, veterans and new recruits alike were under no illusion as to the expectations of their divisional commander.

If it was not going home, the division that had undertaken opposed landings in Morocco and Sicily thought it was the turn of another unit to lead the invasion of France. While Bradley knew the choice of the 1st Division was unjust, he believed it necessary to ensure or at least increase the odds of success. He therefore 'felt compelled to employ the best troops I had' in the invasion of Normandy.[27] As a consequence, the 16th Infantry boarded landing craft for their trip to the beach. Later in the day they would be followed by sister regiments the 18th Infantry in late morning and the 26th Infantry in late afternoon and early evening.

Landings by combat engineers such as the 299th Engineer Combat Battalion who were intended to demolish beach obstacles before they were obscured by rising tide and by Duplex Drive tanks from the 741st Tank Battalion had occurred before or shortly after the arrival of the infantry. (Some of the tanks and engineers appeared in the Capa photographs.) The tanks were expected to arrive before the infantry, and some did but the effort was largely a disaster since few of the tanks were able to 'swim' in due to heavy seas. Private Henry Ferri was unable to describe the damage to his landing craft and memories of his landing on Easy Red.[28]

Most of the engineers were unable to complete their tasks of demolishing the obstacles before the sea rose to cover them during the morning. The 299th Assault Team 12 landed and placed their explosive charges but nineteen engineers and some infantry were killed or wounded when a mortar shell ignited the explosives. Lieutenant Jack Wood was among the wounded.

The 299th Support Team F boat was struck by artillery early in the morning; fifteen of the occupants were killed or wounded.[29] Captain Edwin Perry, one of four or five who reached the shore from that boat, devoted his efforts to organizing engineers on the beach and salvaging explosives. Later in the day he directed obstacle demolition while often exposed to enemy fire. He received the Distinguished Service Cross for his leadership on D-Day.

The experience of the boat sections – with between thirty and thirty-four men in each – from Company F of the 16th between 0630 and 0700 reveals the challenges of landing directly against the German strongpoints:

- Headquarters section landed to the east on Fox Green near strong point WN 62, seventeen men crossed the beach, company executive Lieutenant Pearre among those killed. The company commander Captain Finke was wounded later in the day inland from the beach.
- Section 1 landed on Easy Red, the intended beach, Lieutenant Dennstedt killed, fourteen men crossed.
- Sections 2 and 3 landed on Fox Green, twenty men in each crossed the beach with one-half wounded.
- Section 5 landed on Fox Green near Section 2, Lieutenant Clemens killed, only seven men crossed.
- Section 4 landed on Fox Green 1,100 yards east of Easy Red, all crossed but Lieutenant Siefert was mortally wounded.

The company was badly disorganized and had suffered heavy losses. Yet Sergeant Strojny would lead men in an attack that ultimately assisted in subduing the strong-point WN 61.

E/16th was similarly dispersed, with only one boat section, under Lieutenant John Spaulding landing on Easy Red – apparently with Robert Capa as a passenger. Despite losses to the members of his boat section, the group was fortunate in having crossed some distance to the west of WN 62. They were joined by a few boat sections from Company E of the 116th that landed well to the east of the beaches allocated to the 29th Division. (E/116th was also dispersed and the commander Captain Lawrence Madill was mortally wounded.) These troops, when joined shortly by those of G/16th under Captain Joe Dawson, would form the nucleus of the earliest penetration from the beach on that day.

Attempts to bring historical order to amphibious chaos inevitably simplify reality on the beaches. Very few intact units were sufficiently organized on open beach sections to move inland as a group. Yet just before 1100 in the morning, reports that 'men visible on skyline Easy and Fox believed to be ours'[30] offered glimmers of hope in what seemed an otherwise bleak situation.

The damage sustained by LCI 85 had devastating consequences and was recorded in a dramatic series of photographs associated with two of the most famous photographers along Omaha Beach. Robert Capa described himself as a gambler who decided to land with Company E of the 16th in the first wave.[31]

Some confusion as to his actual landing point may be indicated by the fact that only one Company E boat landed on Easy Red, but that was where Capa contended he landed. He crossed the Channel on the transport *Chase* but Company E departed from the *Henrico*. It is possible that the LCVP stopped at the latter to load troops. Additional confusion exists as to the number of photographs taken by Capa, but the fact remains he was the earliest to disembark with the first wave and his images are among the most remarkable documents of the day.

Coast Guard photographer Robert Sargent was also a passenger in an LCVP from the *Chase*, one that departed slightly later with members of the 1/16th who landed about 0730, or around one hour after the first wave. One of his photographs is the most famous American image from D-Day, but was actually part of a sequence that recorded the run-in to the beach and subsequent events offshore since Sargent remained with the LCVP. In one of the small ironies of the invasion, Sargent and Capa not only departed from the same transport but were linked in the story of the stricken LCI 85. Capa climbed aboard the LCI that had been struck by artillery fire while unloading troops. Sargent exposed photographs of the aftermath of the devastating attempts by LCI 85 to land.

The failure of the medical mission on this portion of Omaha Beach was a result of many contributing factors. According to Major Charles Tegtmeyer, commander of the 16th Infantry Medical Section, one of those factors was the placement of the Collecting Company A of the 1st Medical Battalion on a single vessel, specifically LCI 85, since 'the losses suffered by this group were such that they were rendered non-effective when they were needed most.' He attributed these losses to deliberate fire on the craft carrying personnel wearing the Red Cross brassard. Some of the dead on the vessel, including those from the collecting company, were shown covered with blankets or with faces obscured by censors in the Sargent photos.

The commander of Collecting Company A, Captain Emerald Ralston, acknowledged that his decision to place most of the company on LCI 85 led to many casualties among those who were there to care for and evacuate others. He also believed that the medical group was landed too early when the beach was still unsecured. Generally speaking, LCI were relatively large and vulnerable targets and as such were often not brought in to landing zones until most artillery fire had been eliminated. However, few things worked as planned on D-Day morning on Omaha.

The 16th Infantry Medical Section left the *Chase* on an LCM craft about 0600 and headed for the beach. Obstacles had not been cleared and machine-gun fire was formidable. The coxswain reversed course and landed about 0815 on the western end of Easy Red. The diary of the commander, Major Charles Tegtmeyer, provided a detailed chronicle of conditions on the beach throughout the day, as discussed in Chapter Nine.

Other withering comments were offered, although few so scathing as those of Lieutenant Colonel Charles Horner who commanded the 3rd Battalion (3/16th): 'I personally observed thirty doctors digging foxholes on the beach about 3.00pm. D-day, when hundreds of men were dying on the beach from lack of medical care or else drowning because there was no one other than fighting troops to move them from the in-coming tide.' The doctors and medics had lost their equipment in the surf. Horner believed it 'criminal' that the medical staff did not carry the necessary equipment on their persons.[32]

The earliest penetration inland from the eastern end of Omaha Beach was launched from Easy Red sector. Company G under the command of Captain Joe Dawson landed about 0700 and sustained most of its sixty-three casualties in crossing the beach to the shingle and the ruins of a house. They found remnants of two boat sections from E/116th and the E/16th section of Lieutenant Spaulding. Colonel Marshall later described Dawson as 'an uncommonly accurate witness'.

Dawson organized the available troops and they began to ascend the bluff at a point that would become known as Exit E-2, roughly the location of the modern pathway down to the beach from the Normandy American Cemetery. As Dawson moved up the bluff, he approached and eliminated an enemy machine-gun position. Once the group reached the top of the bluff, Dawson sent the depleted section of Lieutenant Spaulding to attack the unfinished strongpoint WN 64 on the east side of Exit E-1. Company G headed inland towards Colleville-sur-Mer with the E/116th sections in tow. They arrived near a crossroads with the coastal road by about 0900.

Two sections of Company G were ordered to clear a German encampment in woods near the crossroads. The effort required about two hours and cost the company about twelve casualties. By noon a line was formed near the western end of Colleville. The sections that had cleared the woods had moved inland south of the town with some troops from E/116th but they soon encountered enemy resistance along a hedgerow defensive line and fell back. By about 1300 Dawson mounted an effort to move into the town, supported by machine guns from the heavy weapons Company H. They occupied the church and a nearby house before a counter-attack was launched by 3 Company of the 726th Regiment who had been stationed in the town. The 8 Company from the 916th Regiment was also in the vicinity; members of this unit from the 352nd Division were captured by the 16th Infantry on D-Day.

This resistance and fire from bypassed German positions compelled Company G to adopt a nearly circular defensive position at the western end of town. The company lost three killed and two seriously wounded in the attack, with roughly eighteen enemy killed. By mid-afternoon, Dawson estimated his strength at 107 enlisted men and six officers, with an additional twenty-five from other units. Then 'friendly' naval fire from the destroyer USS *Emmons* began about 1530. When it finally ceased at 1700 the church steeple had been toppled and seven or eight more of Dawson's men were casualties; as far as could be determined, no Germans were injured.

American troops continued to advance during the morning and early afternoon. Spaulding and his small section had captured WN 64 later in the morning and then moved inland to join other members of their Company E who had arrived near the coastal road about noon to support Company G. Elements of Company F were also coming through the fields and the three infantry companies of 1/16th advanced inland to the crossroads near the former encampment to support the rear of the Company G position. Perhaps most importantly, the 2nd Battalion of the 18th Infantry had moved through to establish a defensive position on high ground south of the town, a position they held into the morning of the next day (D+1). The 2/18th formed a rectangular defence on three sides and came to realize that enemy troops occupied ground between them and the 16th Infantry, an indication of the fluid tactical landscape in the first days of the invasion.

On the morning of 7 June, Company G completed its sweep through Colleville. A brief engagement occurred in a field on the south edge of town. By mid-morning, five Germans had been killed and twelve surrendered; the short fight had cost an additional two American wounded. Colleville was secure.

(**Above**) The *Samuel Chase* carried members of the 1st Battalion, 16th Infantry to Normandy. Robert Sargent of the Coast Guard was aboard an LCVP from the *Chase* approaching Easy Red shortly after 0700. Each craft carried roughly thirty passengers, so an assault company was divided between six or seven craft. Note the bags intended to protect rifles from sea water. (Image 2 on Colleville 1944; the locations of this and other selected images are indicated on maps in the final chapter.) *(NARA)*

(**Opposite, above**) Smoke was pouring from PA 26-15 on the port side of the craft in which Sargent was located. The LCVP may have been hit by fire from shore, but the smoke was probably generated by a smoke grenade. Various log obstacles were visible in the background. *(NARA)*

(**Opposite, below**) Landing craft 18 and 19 have unloaded their troops. A tremendous pall of smoke obscured much of the sky but the bluff line behind the beach was still visible through the smoke blowing from west to east. *(NARA)*

(**Above**) The 1st Battalion, 16th Infantry begins its invasion of Europe around 0730 as recorded by Sargent in one of the most famous photographs to emerge from World War II. The craft has landed fairly close to shore but the depth of water through which the heavily laden troops must wade is apparent. A disabled Sherman from the 741st Tank Battalion lay on the wide expanse of exposed beach that the infantry had to cross. (*NARA*)

(**Opposite, above**) Landing craft approached the shore while troops who had already landed sheltered behind a veritable forest of sloped pole obstacles. While offering scant protection, such obstacles must have seemed more inviting than moving across the broad expanse of beach while under fire. (Image 1 on Colleville 1944) (*Robert Capa*)
    Robert Capa (*Slightly Out of Focus*, p. 137) stated he landed with Company E, 16th Infantry in the first wave on Easy Red. Only one Company E boat – the section of Lieutenant John Spaulding – landed on that sector. Capa believed (p. 152) that only 8 of 106 negatives survived careless drying during developing in London. In 2014, his former editor John Morris suggested that the original developing may have included several unexposed rolls of 35mm film and no exposed negatives were lost.

(**Opposite, below**) The scene at the edge of the beach. Duplex Drive 'swimming' tanks with exhaust vents and inflated rings are visible on the beach. Most of the DD tanks of the 741st Tank Battalion foundered at sea. One company of tanks was landed near the beach. The infantry sought protection from enemy fire behind the tanks or the iron hedgehogs. The beach obstacles offered the illusion of safety, particularly as the tide rose. The best chance of survival for the assault infantry was to cross the exposed beach to the shingle embankment and if possible to move inland. (*Robert Capa*)

(**Above**) The damaged LCI 85 off Easy Red sector photographed by Sargent on D-Day morning. The 1st Medical Battalion casualty collecting Company A on LCI 85 sustained many casualties themselves which hampered evacuation of wounded from the beach. Capa boarded this vessel after leaving the beach and found the skipper crying at the carnage on his boat (*Slightly Out of Focus*, p. 148). A printed drawing showing the coastline behind Fox Green sector is visible beneath the binoculars at upper right. (*NARA*)

(**Opposite, above**) Company G, 16th Infantry under the command of Captain Joe Dawson pushed inland from Easy Red and established a line west of Colleville by 0900. By noon the company had cleared German soldiers from a bivouac along the coastal highway. Two boat sections from Company E, 116th Infantry that had landed on Easy Red joined the advance. Troops advanced along a roadway towards high ground south of town. They were stopped by German resistance from a field/hedgerow position seen on the east (left) side of the road and fell back to the main line near a crossroads. The road remains unpaved today. (Image location L4 on Colleville 1944)

(**Opposite, below**) Dawson established a U-shaped position at the western end of Colleville. This view from the village churchyard faces north to a portion of the line held by machine guns from Company H, 16th Infantry. After an initial advance at about 1315 that captured the church and a house at the western end of the village, a German counter-attack forced the Americans to adopt a nearly circular position. (Image location L6 on Colleville 1944)

# Chapter Four

# The Photographs of Sergeant Richard Taylor (Fox Red Sector)

Sergeant Richard Taylor was assigned to Detachment L of the 165th Signal Photographic Company and landed at the extreme eastern end of Omaha early on D-Day; his images depict the most evocative faces of the invasion. His captions – rarely if ever published with the photographs – are here reunited with the images.

Most of the soldiers shown in the Taylor photos were members of the 3rd Battalion of the 16th Infantry (3/16th), although patches of the 29th Division indicate that members of Company E of 116th Infantry were mixed with the group. Surviving crewmen from landing craft that had been damaged or destroyed in the landings were also present. Most of the men were soaking wet, having struggled ashore to seek shelter beneath the low stone cliffs. The rising tide also carried in the bodies of those who had drowned in the surf.

The photographs by Taylor are among the most famous from D-Day and provide dramatic images of the human toll of the landings. Nevertheless, much more was happening at the eastern end of Omaha Beach. This was the area allocated to the 3/16th on the morning of the invasion. The four companies of the battalion were carried across the Channel on the *Empire Anvil*. The landing craft headed for Fox Green but as on other sectors the results were mixed.

Company I boats for sections 4 and 5 sank before landing, with the soldiers being transferred to patrol vessels. The other sections were carried to the east by the tide and poor navigation. The commander Captain Richmond managed to redirect various craft that eventually landed about one hour late on Fox Green. Their arrival was not a happy one. The headquarters boat struck a mine, was raked by machine gun and caught fire. The section 1 boat sustained automatic weapon fire and collided with a wooden stake obstacle but was able to withdraw. The boats with sections 2 and 3 were struck by artillery fire and possibly mines, with many casualties in both craft.

Company K landed on Fox Green, with two of the boats being destroyed by mines after landing. The soldiers moved across the beach, but sustained numerous officer casualties in the process. The same artillery shell mortally wounded Captain Prucnal and killed Lieutenant Brandt on the beach. Lieutenant Robinson was shot dead by a sniper. Another officer, Lieutenant Zyblut was seriously wounded. Lieutenant Stumbaugh and Sergeant Barbeiri were able to organize soldiers from sections 1 and 2 and move inland during the morning to form a defensive position on the left of Company L.

Company L lost the section 4 boat and eight men at sea but the other boats arrived on shore around 0700 at Fox Red on the extreme eastern end of Omaha Beach. Most crossed to shelter provided by the cliff shown in the Taylor photographs. Indeed, many of the soldiers present with Sergeant Taylor may have been from this company. It was later calculated that early losses reduced the effectives in the company from 187 to 123 men. Casualties included Captain Armellino who was wounded on the beach; Lieutenant Cutler assumed command. Nevertheless, this company was positioned to begin an advance up a steep ravine that was known to planners as Exit F-1. As such they began the other major movement inland from the eastern end of Omaha Beach.

The German strongpoint WN 60 was placed atop the bluff on the east side of the ravine and it was necessary to reduce this position if the advance was to continue. Lieutenant Jimmie Monteith and section 2 moved up the ravine to begin the assault; the lieutenant directed two tanks firing on the position. Section 3 under Lieutenant Williams advanced up the west side. Support was provided by section 5 and the machine guns from the heavy weapons Company M; some of these soldiers were photographed by Taylor early in the morning. As troops moved up the deep and overgrown ravine, soldiers armed with BARs were suppressing enemy fire from the position. Naval gunfire offshore was falling on the strongpoint; section 2 informed Cutler that it would begin an assault once the naval fire had ceased. At this point he noticed purple smoke indicating other troops had begun to attack. Section 2 was therefore ordered to continue inland where it joined two other sections in establishing the first battalion position on higher ground.

A few Company I soldiers under Lieutenants Kemp and Godwin moved up the ravine but were stopped for a time by the naval gunfire and apparently by Germans who were rolling grenades down the slope. Lieutenant Klenk meanwhile arrived with a mixed band that prepared to join in a landward assault against WN 60. His section 1 from Company L had been reduced on the beach to only twelve men by artillery – probably mortar – fire but Klenk initially moved them west in an attempt to subdue WN 61. The position was defended to such an extent that the group moved back to Fox Red, encountering some of the men from the 116th Infantry who had landed so far to the east. Two soldiers from the 29th Division appear in one of the Taylor photographs.

The outer trenches at WN 60 were overrun; a 75mm gun position, anti-aircraft gun and concrete 'Tobruk' mortar positions were subdued by grenades and satchel charges. Four or five enemy were killed or wounded during the assault before the remainder of the garrison — perhaps thirty-five soldiers — surrendered. The section evidently lost only one soldier to a mine.

By 0900 Cutler informed battalion headquarters that WN 60 had fallen. He again contacted battalion half an hour later to report a position had been established about 600 yards inland near point 62 on a road north-east of the hamlet of Cabourg. A defensive perimeter was formed on this high ground.

Patrols were dispatched southwards to Cabourg. Two groups of three soldiers advanced and disappeared; the small settlement on the eastern end of Colleville-sur-Mer was evidently strongly defended and remained so throughout D-Day. A machine-gun crew consisting of Sergeant Moxley and Privates First Class Demien and Prauener came forward to provide support and likewise disappeared. However, the missing patrol from Company L reappeared the next day on the perimeter of the 2/18th with fifty-two prisoners. The patrol leader Private First Class Mielander spoke German and had convinced the Cabourg garrison to surrender.

Other groups moved eastwards towards Le Grand Hameau. Sergeant Davis led a patrol that cut the road leading back to Colleville then drew enemy fire. They withdrew but returned to the vicinity a second time.

German resistance at WN 60 and the nearby WN 61 had been subdued during the morning, but had by no means ended at the eastern end of Omaha Beach. Cabourg was strongly held by elements of German 726th Infantry (716th Division) and probably troops from a company in the 352nd Division. In addition, various bypassed positions still resisted along the beachfront. A group later estimated of platoon size supported by automatic weapons and mortars launched an attack from the beach area against the rear of the 3/16th position on the high ground. Company L section 2 and headquarters assisted by Stumbaugh's section from Company K and machine guns from Company M defended the position. The Germans sustained an estimated thirteen casualties while the American losses numbered six; Lieutenant Monteith was among the two killed. He was one of three members of the 1st Division to receive the Medal of Honor for actions on D-Day.

The Davis patrol returned once again. Lieutenant Williams then advanced with his section 3 to the outskirts of Le Grand Hameau in the early afternoon where they established the first roadblocks. A reserve group of 104 soldiers from all four companies under Captain Richmond joined them about one hour later. Troops continued to arrive during the afternoon. Some elements of Company K were pinned down by enemy fire in the open fields en route to the village. The company later placed its casualties at fifty-one that day, but noted most had been sustained on the beach.

By evening the battalion commander Lieutenant Colonel Charles Horner had posted the three infantry companies around the town; Company L occupied an orchard about 600 yards to the south-west. Patrols were undertaken into the darkness since the battalion knew it represented the eastern extent of the American bridgehead in Normandy.

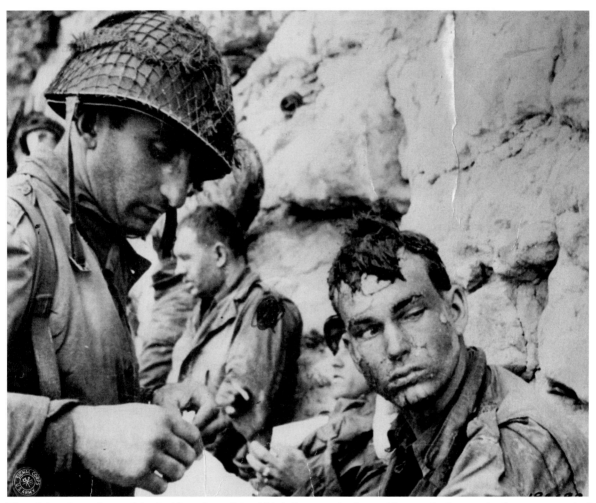

The plight of members of the 3rd Battalion of the 16th Infantry and other soldiers and sailors at the far eastern end of Omaha Beach was dramatically documented in a series of images recorded by army photographer Sergeant Richard Taylor, who landed at approximately 0715 on D-Day. Several of these photographs are well known but were identified by generic Signal Corps captions on 8 June. A subsequent interview with Taylor by the Army Historical Division provided the photographer's captions that included times and map coordinates: 'An American medical officer puts a bandage on the hand of an American soldier who has been injured while landing on the beachhead on the northern coast of France. The man being treated by the medic was burned when a landing craft blew up after hitting a mine. 0845–0900 [time], 698893 [map coordinates].' The soldier has clearly been in the water and the harrowing experience is apparent on his face. The 1st Division shoulder patch of the soldier in the rear has been obscured by a censor. (Image location 4 on Colleville 1944) (NARA)

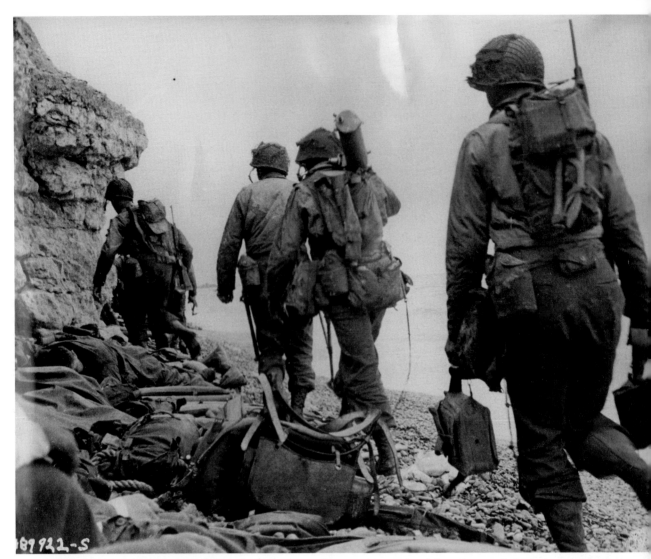

(**Above**) 'American assault troops, members of an infantry unit, carrying full equipment including a machine gun move along a cliff on a beachhead. Vast quantities of equipment brought ashore from landing craft lay at the base of the cliff. The photographer's watch was damaged in the landing, but the times given are considered to be fairly accurate. 0900–0930, 698893.' The heavy machine gun indicates this group was likely associated with Company M, the heavy weapons company in the 3rd Battalion, 16th Infantry. The soldiers are moving west towards the Fox Green sector. (*NARA*)

(**Opposite, above**) 'Men lying on the beach were not there when Sgt. Taylor originally came on the beach. They could have been washed up by water or pulled in by medics. 0930, 698893.' The tide is rising, resulting in less beach exposure; the landings began at 0630, roughly one hour after low tide. The soldier in the foreground appears in the photograph of LCI 83 below. (*NARA*)

(**Opposite, below**) No original caption or subsequent comment was provided. The position of the tide line and the same bodies visible in the above view suggest this image was recorded at roughly the same time. The medic's face expresses the deep concern that must have been commonplace along most sections of Omaha Beach, particularly during the morning. A panorama of the beach is visible in the background. (*NARA*)

189925-S

(**Opposite, above**) The same approximate location along the cliff face in September 2014. Eroded blocks of limestone and shingle cobbles are more visible since the tide has not risen as far.

(**Opposite, below**) 'A group of American assault troops who stormed a beachhead and although wounded gained the comparative safety offered by the chalk cliff at their backs. Food and cigarettes were available to lend comfort to the men. Time uncertain. These men had been burned by explosion of mines. Note medic tags.' (*NARA*)

(**Above**) A close-up view of a group along the cliff face. The two soldiers at right have the 29th Division patch on their jackets; members of the 116th Infantry from that division were landed far to the east of their intended beach sectors. Some advanced inland with the 16th Infantry while others joined the displaced soldiers on Fox Red. M1 rifles are shown against the cliff. A soldier holds an M1 carbine with a folding stock designed for airborne troops. The carbine is partially disassembled for drying and cleaning. (*NARA*)

'The man on the right had not been wounded but was suffering from nervous shock. On the extreme left and in the background can be seen an LST [LCT] which had blown up with its cargo of three ammunition trucks after hitting a mine. 1100, 710891.' The injured soldier is receiving plasma. (*NARA*)

'Wounded man awaiting to be evacuated' [no time or coordinates]. The medic is filling out a casualty tag. One of the inflatable life belts that appear so frequently in D-Day photographs is visible. (*NARA*)

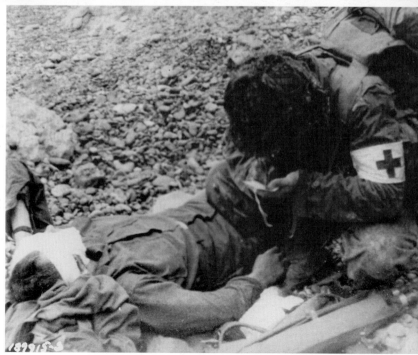

No original caption was provided. Medics administering plasma to wounded soldier who is not visible. The 1st Division patch is barely visible on the sleeve of the sergeant in the foreground. (NARA)

No original caption, time or coordinates. A scene with one soldier wrapped in a blanket and another lying nearby. An inflated life belt is visible between the men. (NARA)

189923-S

The entrance tunnel led to a concrete mortar Tobruk position at WN 60 facing into Exit F-1. (Image location L1 facing north-west on Colleville 1944)

(**Opposite, above**) 'This ship came into shore despite the mines it hit. Troops disembarking are engineer troops. Note hole in ship's hull at water level below the marking US 83 caused by mine explosion. The ship was also hit by enemy 88 fire – note hole on port side next to number on the deck – it is difficult to see because of the personnel aboard ship. The equipment that has landed is in front of the draw where engineers built road. In the background can be seen smoke from the far end of beach where fighting is taking place. Approximately 1300, looking down beach towards Pointe du Hoe [Hoc] from approximately 695894.' (Image location 5 on Colleville 1944) (*NARA*)

Bernage argued the time was earlier, most likely around 1130. The bare-headed soldier at lower left appears in the photograph on page 71 (top) taken at 0930. LCI 83 was damaged although probably not by an 88mm gun. The 88 casemate at WN 61 had been eliminated early in the day and the one at WN 72 was focused on landings on the Dog Beach sectors. Engineers began opening a road up Exit F-1 in the late afternoon/early evening. By midnight Shermans from the 745th Tank Battalion had moved up the road to support the 16th Infantry troops inland.

(**Opposite, below**) Open fields facing south-east from WN 60 above Fox Red. The 3/16th Infantry subdued WN 60 on the morning of D-Day and established a command post near this location. Elements of several companies advanced across this now open landscape during the afternoon and early evening to form the eastern flank of the bridgehead at Sainte-Honorine. (Image location L1 facing south-east on Colleville 1944)

# Chapter Five

# Beach Landings and Views

The 29th Division was the first divisional infantry unit to cross the Atlantic to Europe, arriving in England in 1942. These National Guard regiments were raised in Virginia and Maryland but with officers and men from various states by D-Day. Company F of the 116th Infantry originated in the South Boston area of Virginia, but one of the officers, Lieutenant Matthew Daley, was from Philadelphia and the company executive Lieutenant Ernest Wise was a resident of Baltimore. Nevertheless, a core of officers and men from Virginia in the 116th Infantry and Maryland in the 115th and 175th Infantry regiments would land in Normandy. A fourth regiment – the 176th originally from the Richmond/Petersburg region of Virginia – had been with the division but was transferred out in 1942[33] during the 'triangulation' reduction within army divisions to three regiments each with three battalions.

The division had been commanded by the popular Leonard Gerow from Petersburg, but upon his promotion to command of V Corps the 29th inherited a regular army martinet Charles Gerhardt with strong views on discipline and leadership. He was determined to stamp his mark on the soldiers and despite his strict ways had supporters in the division. Bradley described him as a 'peppery' cavalry officer whose enthusiasm at times overcame his military judgement.[34] Under his leadership the division showed innovation in addressing the problem of combat exhaustion and he also created then defended the short-lived (five hours!) divisional brothel in Brittany known as the Corral.[35]

The assault on the western half of Omaha Beach was led by the 116th Infantry, the 5th Ranger Battalion and a portion of the 2nd Ranger Battalion. (Three other companies of the 2nd Rangers were climbing the cliffs at Pointe du Hoc that morning.) As with other units that day, the location and timing of the landings made all the difference in terms of survival and ability to proceed inland. The worst locations were obviously opposite the beach exits. A paved road led from the Dog Green sector through Exit D-1 into the village of Vierville. The exit was blocked by a concrete wall and defended by strongpoints both on the eastern bluff (WN 71) and to the west at WN 73. A concrete emplacement (WN 72) at the blocking wall sheltered an 88mm gun designed to fire laterally eastwards along the beach. WN 72 also contained a double embrasure casemate mounting a 50mm gun and machine guns.

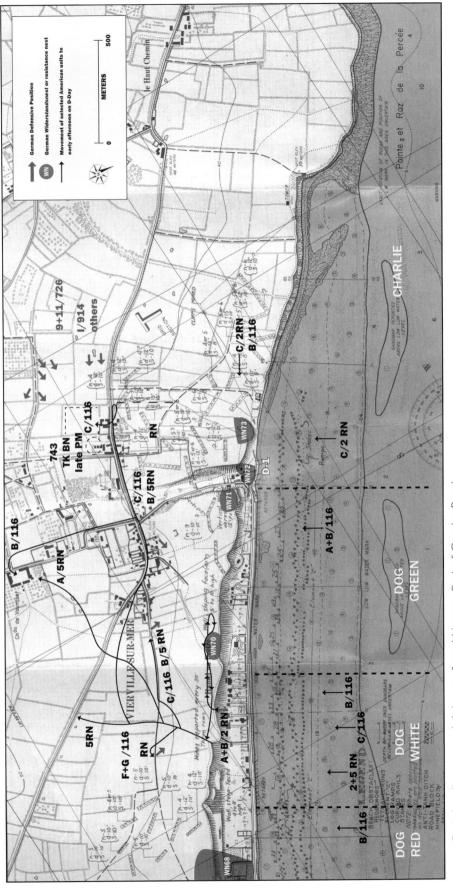

Early Landings on and Advance from Western End of Omaha Beach.

Company C of the 2nd Rangers arrived with the first wave around 0645, landing on Dog Green and the adjacent Charlie sector. More than half of the company – thirty-five of sixty-four – became casualties including Sergeant Walter Geldon (see Chapter One). Two other 2nd Ranger companies and the 5th Rangers landed further to the east on Dog White with relatively few losses and were positioned to participate in the first major movement inland from this end of Omaha Beach.

No infantry unit suffered more heavily on Omaha Beach than did Company A of the 116th Infantry. The landing craft carrying the section of Lieutenant Garing was lost at sea about 1,000 yards from the beach; these soldiers were fortunate in as much as some were rescued. The other craft made the Dog Green shore directly opposite Exit D-1 and WN 71 and 72, the most strongly defended point on the beach.

The heavy guns of the strongpoints were not needed; mortars and machine guns firing from the cliff directly into the company did the damage. Lieutenant Clyde Tidrick was killed and Lieutenant Ray Nance wounded on the beach. No bomb or shell craters were present and attempts to establish a firing line on the beach were futile. Members of one boat section that included company commander Captain Taylor Fellers, Lieutenant Benjamin Kearfott and thirty men were all killed.

The destruction had occurred quickly; survivors described the company as inert and leaderless within ten minutes. By the time elements of Company B landed behind them, it was estimated that only one-third of the soldiers were uninjured. Company A had been effectively destroyed. Thirty members of the company were residents of the Bedford area in western Virginia; nineteen of them were killed in the water or on the beach while four others were rescued from the landing craft that sank.

Ray Nance, who died in Bedford decades later, came to know the guilt of a survivor. As a postman he repeatedly visited many of the family homes of his former soldiers, including those who died offshore or on the beach. He felt 'a little twinge of guilt' about returning alive and wondered if the families somehow resented his survival.[36]

Companies B and D of the 116th also had difficult landings. Those troops that landed on Dog Green suffered much of what befell Company A. Casualties were high in Company B and included Captain Ettore Zappacosta who was killed in the water. The heavy weapons Company D lost their commander Captain Walter Schilling when an artillery shell struck the bow of the landing craft while it was still hundreds of yards offshore. Some boat sections from Company B landed on Dog White, as did all of Company C which enjoyed the best landings by far of the battalion.

Tragic events on this end of the beach included the destruction of landing craft. LCI 91 that carried elements of the 116th headquarters group was approaching Dog White sector when it was struck by artillery or mines. The carnage was appalling. All who occupied the forward compartment were lost.

Soldiers and sailors jumped overboard to escape the damage; one unfortunate soldier carrying a flamethrower was himself blown overboard in flames. The vessel burned for the remainder of D-Day and presented a sight that no one on the beach would forget.[37]

Brigadier General Norman Cota was the assistant commander of the 29th Division and emerged as one of the legendary figures of the American D-Day landings. He was fortunate to land at Dog White at about 0730 on one of the relatively undefended portions of the beach. His aide Lieutenant Jack Shea landed with Cota's staff and provided a record of unparalleled value.

Cota exerted his leadership from the outset. When informed that members of the 5th Ranger Battalion were intermingled with troops from his own division, Cota urged the Rangers to 'lead the way'. In reality, C/116th and the Rangers ascended the cliff and proceeded inland at about the same time. It was only the first of several memorable quotations by the general on that day. (Legends can, however, occasionally be deceiving. The statement 'Only two types of men will remain on this beach – the dead and those who are going to die' attributed to Cota in the film *The Longest Day* was in fact uttered by Colonel George Taylor to motivate 16th Infantry troops at the opposite end of Omaha.)

Company C reached the shore about 1,000 yards east of their intended landing point but did so in a fairly compact group. Their landing area was near the point where LCI 91 later burst into flames. The various boat sections crossed the beach to a low timber sea wall and were confronted by wire obstacles behind the beachfront road. Cota urged the leader of section 1 Robert Bedell to move forward: 'Well, lieutenant … We've got to get them off the beach. We've got to get them moving.'[38]

Private Ingram Lambert went forward to place a Bangalore torpedo to blow a gap in the wire. Lambert was probably the soldier cut down by machine-gun fire; he called out for a medic and then for his mother before dying. Lieutenant Stanley Schwartz went forward and ignited the charge. The company moved through the resulting gap and a second opening onto the flat that led to the slope up the bluff. They passed a complex of trenches and moved through tall grass and bushes to the base of the slope.

Troops ascending the slope represented a mixture from Company C, boat sections from other companies, Rangers from the 5th Battalion, and later the 2nd Battalion. The first troops up to the bluff were probably Lieutenant Bedell's section. They passed through smoke from burning vegetation and by a concrete foundation near the crest shown in the view recorded by Weintraub on 25 June. Several German prisoners were heading down the slope. Upon reaching the beach, one was wounded by a German machine gun. He dropped to his knees and was killed by another burst of fire from a position on the bluff.

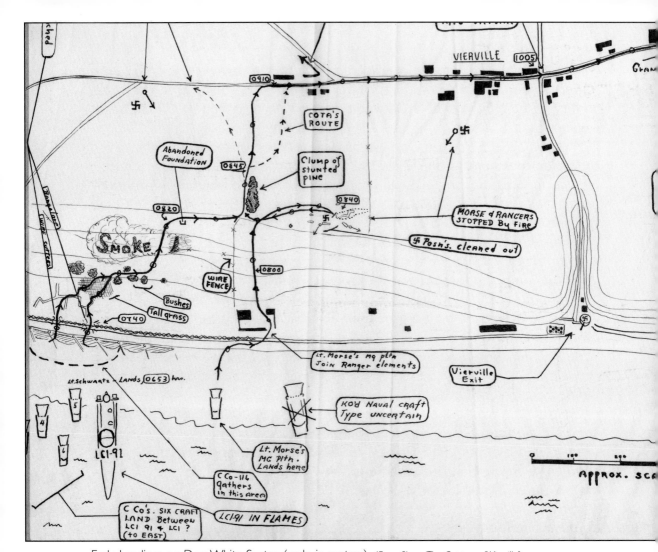

Early Landings on Dog White Sector (scale in metres). *(From Shea, 'The Capture of Vierville')*

As the men began to move past a stand of small pine trees onto the flat and open landscape of the bluff, machine-gun fire from several positions made movement difficult. Cota had moved up from the beach and secured three Ranger volunteers to go after one particularly troublesome position near the small inland road between Les Moulins and Vierville. One Ranger was killed while attacking the position but the others returned with the gun. Bedell and his section then began to move up to the inland road with some Rangers, to be followed by Cota on a slightly different route.

A boat section from Company D commanded by Lieutenant Verne Morse linked up with some Rangers and moved westwards to attack and subdue the enemy position WN 70. Morse described the position as containing communication trenches, weapons pits with machine guns and dugout shelters for the defenders. The

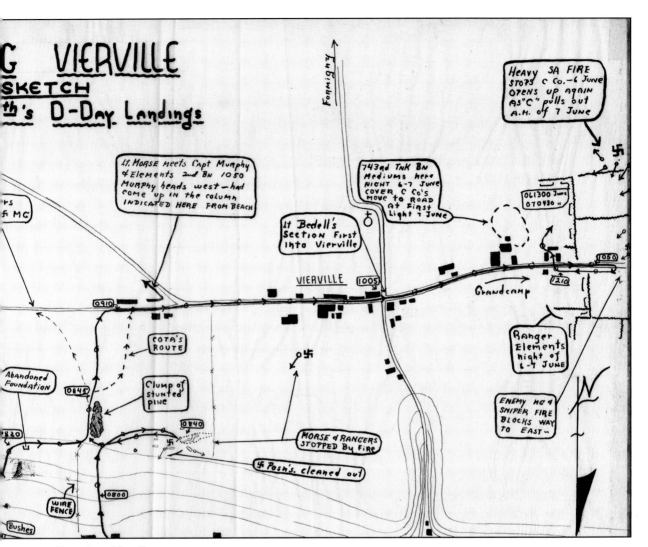

Entry into Vierville. *(From Shea, 'The Capture of Vierville')*

strongpoint also contained two 75mm guns – one in a concrete casemate – and mortars.[39] They overran the trenches and shelters, taking about fifteen prisoners including two who popped up behind Morse fully armed but claiming to be foreigners compelled into German service. The group tried to continue westwards but were stopped at a wire fence by machine-gun fire in the vicinity of Vierville. They returned to the place where they had climbed the bluff to find the 116th Infantry command group. Taking the opportunity to unburden themselves of the prisoners to the command group, they then followed the route across the field to the road leading to Vierville.

Company C and the Rangers entered the crossroads at Vierville between 1000 and 1100, demonstrating once again that manoeuvre from less heavily defended beach sectors was the key to success – and lower casualties – that day on Omaha.

A group from Company B under Lieutenant Taylor moved through the crossroads inland to the stone-walled Chateau de Vaumicel. They defended this impromptu fortress against a German counter-attack and were reinforced by Rangers. During the afternoon, Taylor led his group south then west about 600 yards, advancing inland a greater distance than any other from the division before returning to the 1st Battalion area late in the evening.

Shortly after noon, members of C/116th and B/5th Rangers were ordered to advance westwards by General Cota. The movement did not progress very far beyond the western limits of the village before encountering machine-gun fire from hedgerow positions. Company C lost Private First Class James Page wounded, and three killed: Staff Sergeant Ted Mouray, Private First Class Leo King and Lieutenant Schwartz who led his section forward through the wire earlier in the day. Members of the company subdued one machine-gun position but were halted by small-arms fire. Support from tanks that had come up from the beach was required to extricate the company as it withdrew to join the general advance early on the morning of 7 June.[40]

The Rangers were also stymied in their attempts to move forward. Plans to stage an advance towards Pointe du Hoc to relieve their fellow Rangers were cancelled in the evening. One platoon from A/5th Rangers left the Chateau de Vaumicel and slipped through fields to arrive at Pointe du Hoc about dusk.

Exit D-3 at Les Moulins was another difficult place to land, being flanked by the two strongpoints WN 66 and WN 68. The first wave landing of 2/116th again met with variable success, as reflected in the experiences of Companies F and G. The three sections from G that landed on the eastern edge of Dog Red sector sustained relatively few casualties on the beach and achieved one of the fastest concentrations early on D-Day. The three sections from F also landed to the right of D-3 and some soldiers commented that no fire was encountered until they were halfway across the beach. On the other hand, it seemed to Sergeant Walter Wilborn they 'were hit hard by everything [the] Germans had'. Sections from both companies that landed to the west on Dog Red continued to move westwards and eventually joined with some Rangers on the inland movement from Dog White sector.[41]

For the sections from both companies that landed on Easy Green on the east side of D-3, the levels of resistance and loss were greater. One Company G section lost about half of its men simply crossing the beach. Lieutenant Matt Daley from section 2 of Company F urged the coxswain of his boat to continue forward until beaching; the section left the boat with dry feet but Daley was wounded in the hand crossing the beach. (After using a morphine syrette he bandaged his wound, then smeared sand to darken the bandage thinking the white color would make him a target).[42] The company commander William Callahan was wounded on the beach, ending his participation in the war. The company executive officer Lieutenant Ernest Wise reached the sea wall but was killed near Lieutenant Daley shortly afterwards. The portions of the

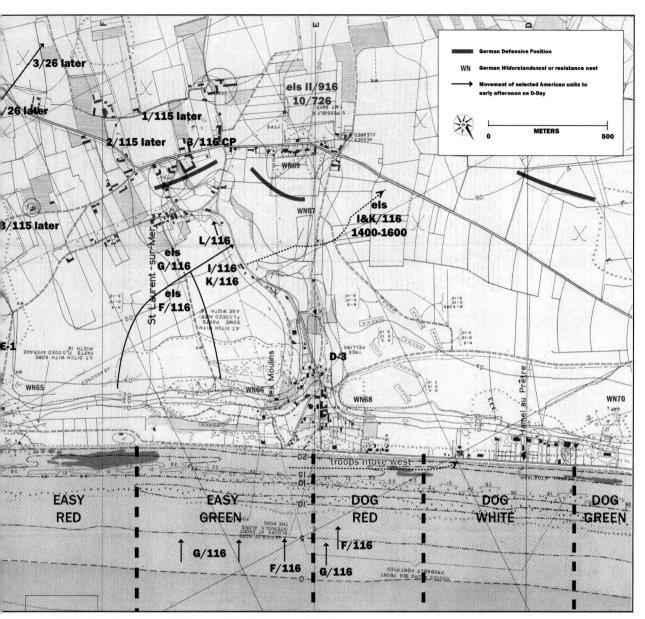

Early Landings on and Advance Inland near Les Moulins.

companies that landed to the east joined the efforts to subdue the defenses facing the beach at Les Moulins and then moved inland towards Saint-Laurent-sur-Mer.

Naval gunfire performed a vital role all along the beach sectors. Two destroyers – probably USS *Thompson* and *Carmick* – moved in close to shore to place heavy fire on the Les Moulins exit during the morning and later in the day.[43]

Two first-hand accounts illustrate the diversity of experiences on Omaha Beach during D-Day afternoon. Chet Hansen accompanied the First Army Chief of Staff William Kean to the beach – probably at Easy Red – in the early afternoon of D-Day to provide Bradley with an assessment of conditions. They left USS *Augusta* on a PT boat and transferred to an LCVP about 2,000 yards offshore for the trip to the beach.

> There on Omaha Beach lay a heavy pile of rubble with the wrecked boats, their backs broken in the low water. There were innumerable tetrahedrons, hedge-rows [hedgehogs] with teller mines fastened to the tops of the steel or iron obstacles. Work was proceeding slowly in the removing of the obstacles. There were some small arms fire to the beach on our right, but the troops in front were just beginning to get the exit from the beach in operating order. A single file of troops was passing up the hill to the left in a clear path through a mine-field. The path had been indicated by white tape. There were a score of dead troops on the beach, sprawling and wet, lying where they had fallen. No one had yet collected the dead. Off near the sea row there were fifteen or twenty wounded receiving care from a battalion surgeon.[44]

A more harrowing image was presented by Major Stanley Bach, the 1st Division liaison to the 29th Division who landed at about 1000 on the Easy Green beach sector. His entries provided some of most stark accounts of life and death on Omaha Beach that day as indicated in excerpts:[45]

> 1200 – Noon – beach high tide, bodies floating … many dead Americans on beach at High Water Mark …
>
> 1320 – Saw direct hit on beached LCM, flames everywhere, men burning alive. Beach now can be seen by aid of glasses entire distance about 2 miles east and 2 miles west – with tide slowly going out – long runnels appear also obstacles with deadly teller mines on top of beach.
>
> 1400 – Fire on beach increasing – aid man goes to help man that was machine-gunned but hit by bullet himself, another aid man pulled him back to fox-hole …
>
> 1440 – More mortar fire and more men hit – LCVP unload five loads of men, they lie down on beach, mortar fire kills five of them – rest up and run for fox holes we left couple of hours ago …
>
> 1600 – We reach wood through field 500 yards from top of cliff we just came up. See man on knees, we think he is praying or scared, roll him over and he is dead, died on knees praying.

Norman Cota was the most peripatetic soldier on Omaha Beach throughout D-Day. After moving into Vierville late in the morning and enduring the naval shelling of the village, he instructed Rangers and C/116th to begin an advance westwards. Cota then headed down Exit D-1 towards the Dog Green sector of the beach that had been a killing field just hours before. He moved past the machine-gun embrasures of WN 71 that faced into the ravine, described by Shea as the 'caves', from which more than fifty Germans would emerge to surrender. They moved eastwards along the beach-front where Shea noted thirty to fifty bodies roughly every 100 yards. Cota ordered engineers to clear the concrete walls from the entrance to D-1 to permit vehicle traffic to move off the beach.

By mid-afternoon his group had moved past D-3 to the 1st Division command post behind the WN 65 strongpoint at E-1. He then moved up to the Saint-Laurent area to direct the actions of the 115th Infantry, ordering the 3rd Battalion to attack a strongpoint near the village that evening or the following morning. He moved back towards the beach to meet with General Clarence Huebner of the 1st Division, where he learned the 29th Division had established its headquarters in a quarry in Exit D-1 near Vierville. His group then moved back to the western end of Omaha Beach to meet with General Gerhardt to plan the advance for the division's three regiments. Darkness had fallen and blankets were being removed from the dead to cover the wounded. A casualty collecting point had been established near the now-demolished wall at the entrance to D-1. Burning landing craft including LCI 91 illuminated the beach and those soldiers moving along it were compelled to stay close to the sea wall to avoid becoming visible to snipers.

A memorial service at the first American cemetery on Omaha Beach photographed by Weintraub on 25 June 1944. The view recorded the appearance of the bluff slope behind Dog White sector in the area where Company C of the 116th Infantry, the Rangers and General Norman Cota ascended the slope beginning around 0800. Private Ingram Lambert placed a Bangalore torpedo to blow a gap in the wire but was killed by machine-gun fire. Lieutenant Stanley Schwartz ignited the charge to create an opening. The grass at the base of the slope and the concrete foundation were mentioned in accounts of D-Day morning by Lieutenant Jack Shea. (Image location L15 facing south-west on St Laurent 1944) (NARA)

THIS MARKS
THE SITE
OF FIRST
AMERICAN
CEMETERY
IN FRANCE
WORLD WAR II
SINCE
MOVED TO
AMERICAN
CEMETERY N°1

(**Above**) A modern view of this portion of Dog White sector with the marker commemorating the first cemetery on the beach.

(**Opposite, above**) A modern view facing west above Dog White and along the bluff past the site of WN 70. The first troops to exit the western portion of Omaha Beach moved inland near this location to advance west to Vierville. (Image location L17 on St Laurent 1944)

(**Opposite, below**) This modern view faces north-east from the junction of an unpaved farm lane with the road to Vierville. Wheat fields on the bluff were mentioned in several company accounts. Many of the troops advanced through agricultural fields near this lane to enter Vierville around 1000 on D-Day. (Image location L18 on St Laurent 1944)

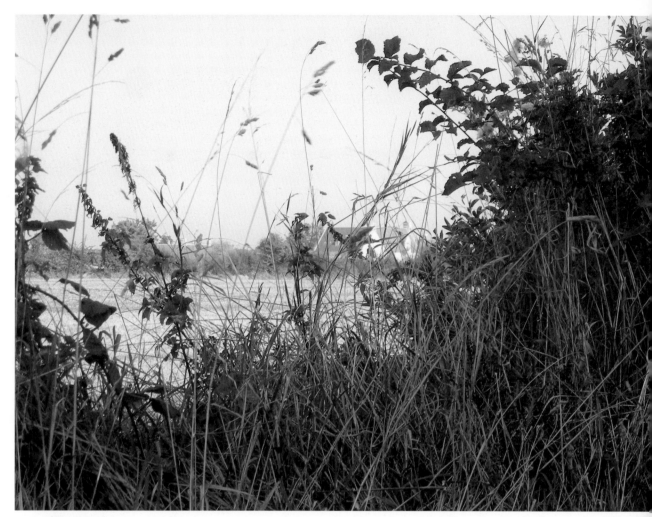

(**Above**) An enemy machine gun was positioned along this hedgerow facing the western edge of Vierville. Machine-gun fire killed three soldiers and wounded one from Company C as they advanced during the afternoon. Among those killed were Staff Sergeant Ted Mouray, Private First Class Leo King and Lieutenant Schwartz who had breached the wire to permit troops to ascend the bluff from Dog White earlier in the day. The company reduced the machine-gun positions during the afternoon but was ordered by the commander of 1/116th to hold in place for reorganization. Their movement early on 7 June required covering fire provided by the 743rd Tank Battalion that had come up from the beach on the evening of D-Day. (Image location L23 on Vierville 1944)

(**Opposite, above**) The ruined LCI 91 lying on the sand with tide out, showing extensive damage on the starboard side that had faced WN 72. LCI 91 carried the alternate headquarters for the 116th Infantry to the beach. The vessel, struck by artillery and possibly mines, burned throughout the day. No one in the forward compartment escaped, due to the artillery impact that is clearly visible. (*Bernard Lebrec*)

(**Opposite, below**) An LCVP with infantry attributed by Georges Bernage to Company H of the 116th Infantry (*Omaha Beach*, pp. 108–9) approaches Easy Red east of Exit E-1 about 0730 on D-Day. The soldiers are armed with M1 carbines and M1903 rifles. The distinctive smoke column on the beach appears in several photographs. (Image location 3 on Colleville 1944) (*NARA*)

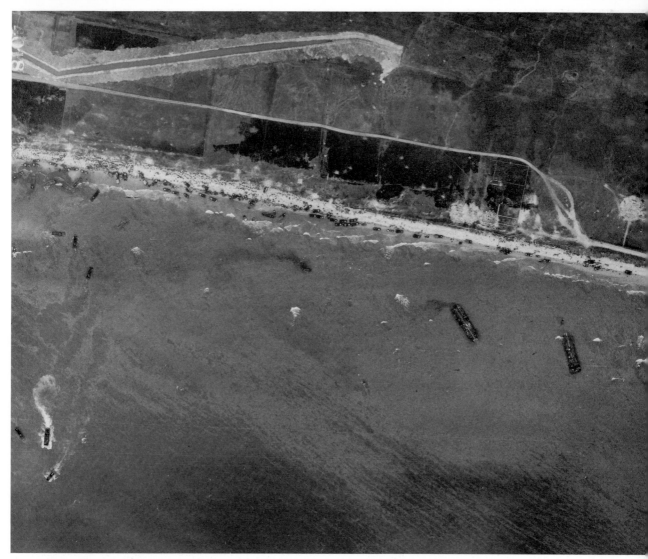

(**Above**) View of Easy Red/Green sectors of Omaha Beach showing landing of 18th Infantry and 115th Infantry west of Exit E-1 around noon on D-Day. (Image location 9 on St Laurent 1944) *(NARA)*

(**Opposite, above**) The modern landscape showing housing development including construction on the site of the anti-tank ditch visible in the previous photograph on the inland side of the road. *(Google Earth)*

(**Opposite, below**) Captain Herman Wall, commander of the 165th Signal Photographic Company, recorded the landings on Easy Red between exits E-3 and E-1. [National Archives 111-SC-189988]. Landing craft from assault transports approach the beach with LCIs.

(**Opposite, above**) LCIs 490 and 496 standing off Exit E-3 near midday. The lower concrete casemate of WN 62 and the house used by the German garrison are visible at right. (Image location 6 on Colleville 1944) (*NARA*)

(**Opposite, below**) A landing craft approaches the shore; censors have marked the background to be deleted. (*NARA*)

(**Above**) Troops begin unloading on a beach sector, probably Easy Red east of E-1, at midday judging by the shadows. The photograph was one of a series by Captain Wall who landed about 1130 in the morning (Thompson and Harris, *The Signal Corps: The Outcome*, p.112). (Image location 7 on Colleville 1944) (*NARA*)

(**Above**) An excellent Navy view of Company C, 115th Infantry using the bow ramps to disembark from LCI 412 onto Dog Red sector in the later morning of D-Day. A 29th Division shoulder patch is visible at base of stairs. (Image location 12 on St Laurent 1944) *(NARA)*

(**Opposite, above**) The 115th Infantry disembark from LCIs 553 and 410 onto Easy Red around midday on 6 June. The distinctive smoke column to the west near E-1 is visible. (Image location 8 facing south-west on Colleville 1944) *(NARA)*

(**Opposite, below**) A detailed view of LCI 553, which carried the headquarters group from the 2nd Battalion, 115th Infantry. The LCI was damaged and abandoned on the beach. Early in the morning on 10 June, this battalion was attacked near Lison; the position was overrun and their commander Lieutenant Colonel William Warfield was killed. (Image location 8 facing south-west on Colleville 1944) *(NARA)*

(**Opposite, above**) LCVP PA 26-28 and the beached LCI 553 are shown west of WN 62 that is visible in the background. After recording this photograph, Captain Wall was seriously wounded. He was evacuated to a hospital ship but managed to save his camera and its precious film (Thompson and Harris, *The Signal Corps: The Outcome*, p. 112). This location was close to the point where Company G and elements of Company E of the 16th Infantry began to move inland early on D-Day morning. (Image location 8 facing south-east on Colleville 1944) (*NARA*)

(**Opposite, below**) The modern view from approximately the same position on the beach.

(**Above**) View through porthole past anti-aircraft mount to shore at Exit E-1, Easy Red sector. The image was probably recorded shortly after D-Day. Vehicles were moving up the right (west) side of the exit and landing craft were visible on the beach. WN 65 was visible near the road at right, while the unfinished WN 64 stood near the top of the slope at left. (Image location L12 on St Laurent 1944) (*NARA*)

(**Opposite, above**) The great Channel storm of late June did considerable damage to the artificial Mulberry harbours at Omaha and on the British Gold Beach at Arromanches. This photograph was recorded by Weigle during the period 19–21 June. *(NARA)*

(**Opposite, below**) A portion of the Omaha harbour was photographed by Rosenblum on 23 June. Although the jetties projecting from the shore appear intact, the harbour structure sustained considerable damage and was abandoned in favour of direct unloading onto the beach. *(NARA)*

(**Above**) View facing west of Omaha Beach with Exit D-3 at junction of Easy Green/Dog Red sectors visible at upper left. Elements of the Mulberry harbour – the line of ships intended to provide a breakwater – are visible. *(NARA)*

An offshore view of the air strip behind Easy Red and Green beaches between exits E-1 and D-3. The state of the harbour and development of the air strip suggest a time after 20 June when the great sea storm destroyed much of the harbour. *(NARA)*

# Chapter Six

# Utah Beach and Coastal Defences

The landings on the Utah Beach sectors occurred opposite causeway Exit 2 at Les Dunes de Madeleine roughly 2,000 yards south-east of the intended location. The landscape was completely different than that found at Omaha, with low-lying sand dunes backed by wetlands. Exits from the beach were thus elevated causeways leading to the inland villages on higher ground.

The landings on Utah were largely unopposed, although artillery fire continued to fall on the beaches. The mistaken landings had the advantage of unloading the troops on a sector that was less heavily defended than the planned one. No lasting impact arose from the initial unloading of the troops, due in part to leadership decisions made by Brigadier General Theodore Roosevelt, assistant commander of the 4th Division, who landed with the assault troops. Roosevelt would die of illness in Normandy, but was awarded the Medal of Honor for decisions made on Utah Beach. Illness and exhaustion were common among some older officers during the campaign.

The Utah landings by the American VII Corps represented not only the western flank of the Allied beachhead but were also isolated from Omaha and the British/ Canadian beaches by a considerable distance. Indeed, the estuary of the River Douve lay between the Cotentin Peninsula where Utah was located and the remainder of the coastline on which the Allied beaches were situated.

This isolation and the threat of enemy reaction were the primary reasons Omar Bradley insisted on the deployment of the airborne divisions inland from Utah Beach. The landings of the 4th Infantry Division were alternately protected by and then expected to provide relief for parachute and glider landings inland by the airborne divisions. The importance of relief by the seaborne forces was impressed upon the paratroopers in Sainte-Mère-Église who had heard no definitive information until late evening on D-Day that the landings had even taken place, leading to rumours among the soldiers that they were on their own. However, just before 1900 the 2/505th reported contact with Company A of the 8th Infantry.[46]

Various elements of the 101st had secured beach causeways and soon encountered troops from the 8th Infantry moving inland. Others such as Colonel Howard

Johnson of the 501st near Angoville-au-Plain heard a midday broadcast from the BBC on 6 June that the landings had taken place and were going according to plan. Johnson was able to use the radio of his naval fire control officer to direct gunfire from the USS *Quincy* on inland German batteries.[47]

Movement inland occurred rapidly. The 8th Infantry advanced westwards to Les Forges on the highway between Carentan and Sainte-Mère-Église, establishing positions in the general area where glider landings would occur that evening and again early on 7 June. The 3/8th Infantry was accompanied by a composite force of tanks, reconnaissance armoured cars and infantry under the command of Colonel Edson Raff that attempted to move northwards from the Les Forges crossroads on the evening of 6 June. The force sought to clear the glider landing area in the vicinity but was unable to do so when roughly sixty or more towed gliders carrying 82nd Division artillery and other units arrived at about 2100 in the evening. German defensive positions on elevated ground to the north, lying between Les Forges and Sainte-Mère-Église, opened fire on the gliders and made organized landings impossible. Casualties resulted from the difficult landings.[48]

The 22nd Infantry sent one battalion up the coast to attack the successive beach defensive positions, while the other two marched inland to assist the 502nd Parachute Infantry in securing the north-eastern face of the bridgehead near Foucarville. The third regiment in the 4th Division, the 12th Infantry, landed later in the day and moved up on the left flank of the 22nd Infantry to the area near Beuzeville-au-Plain. They would establish a united front with the 82nd Division the following day.

The results on 7 June were mixed but on the whole the American position on the Cotentin was organized and solidified. The 8th Infantry advanced northwards against the strong German position north of Les Forges. Additional landings carrying the 325th Glider Infantry occurred early that morning and it is these landings that are likely shown in the photograph in Chapter Two. The 3/8th Infantry had a difficult time crossing a stream and moving up the highway against this opposition. The 2nd Battalion moved against Écoqueneauville shortly after the 1st Battalion began an advance on Turqueville. Both were successful, the 2nd being aided by Sergeant John Svonchek who was a prisoner of the 795th Ost Battalion. When he realized the battalion was composed of troops from Georgia, Svonchek spoke to them in Russian and convinced some to give up the fight, which in turn led to the wholesale surrender of the unit.

The 2nd Battalion then moved up to Sainte-Mère-Église just in time to aid the 82nd Airborne in an advance against enemy positions north of the town. The 8th Infantry moved up one side of the highway while Vandervoort's 2/505th advanced with supporting armour along the other side. Tanks from the 746th Battalion had earlier aided in halting an enemy armoured advance on the town from the north, then in turn moved up the road to Neuville-au-Plain, where Lieutenant Turnbull and members of D/505th had held on the day before. Other American tanks entered the town, capturing prisoners and freeing paratroops probably from Turnbull's platoon. The armour then withdrew since they lacked infantry support and Neuville again reverted to enemy control.[49] Such back-and-forth movement was common in the first days of the invasion on the northern edge of the Cotentin beachhead.

In addition to creating defensive positions along the probable landing beaches and coasts, the Germans had built numerous positions mounting large artillery pieces that could fire on beaches and Allied shipping. They were sited either on coastal promontories or on headlands slightly inland from the coast.

Pointe du Hoc was one such location on a small peninsula west of Omaha Beach. The position had been bombed by the Air Corps but it was believed the batteries remained intact. The 2nd Ranger Battalion practised scaling cliffs in England before the invasion and adapted specialized equipment such as London Fire Brigade ladders and ropes attached to rocket-propelled grappling hooks to aid them in ascending the cliffs that were about ninety feet high. They would also be supported by naval gunfire from the destroyers USS *Satterlee* and HMS *Talybont* directed at machine-gun positions on the cliffs. Three Ranger companies climbed the east cliff on D-Day morning only to discover the heavy 155mm howitzers had yet to be mounted in the concrete casemates. The artillery pieces were later found in an orchard a few miles inland and destroyed. Some Rangers marched from Vierville to the Pointe in the evening but the force remained isolated for two days until relief arrived from the 29th Division and associated armoured forces, by which time their numbers had been severely reduced by casualties.[50]

The batteries at Crisbecq and Azeville on the Cotentin were functional and caused considerable concern. These positions had been bombed but continued to fire upon the beaches and invasion fleet. Crisbecq mounted three heavy 210mm guns of Czech manufacture, two of which were placed in substantial concrete casemates. The battery had smaller gun and defensive positions and underground ammunition magazines connected to the guns by communication trenches. Those guns were manned by the Kriegsmarine or naval personnel and the position was defended by a company from the 919th Regiment of the 709th Division. Azeville was partially within the village of that name and contained four camouflaged concrete blockhouses with 150mm guns again connected by communication trenches to underground magazines. The battery was protected by machine guns, minefields and barbed wire entanglements.

The 4th Division sought to move north to the objective line planned for D-Day and launched attacks on both positions on 7 June. The 2/22nd advanced against Azeville while the 1/22nd moved into the village of Saint-Marcouf while advancing on Crisbecq. The members of the 1st Battalion were therefore the first Americans to see the effects of the errant Allied bombing on the night of 5-6 June. Both attacks were repulsed; the Americans moved back down the coast and the Germans returned to Saint-Marcouf that evening. The Americans resumed the attack on 8 June but with much the same result. Saint-Marcouf was reoccupied, as reflected in the photographic series in Chapter Seven, but the 1/22nd again fell back to positions south of the village in the evening and the 2/22nd recoiled in reaction to a counter-attack from Azeville.

The Azeville battery was finally subdued on the afternoon of 9 June by the 3/22nd but Crisbecq remained in German possession. The latter position had been the focus of naval and artillery fire and was temporarily bypassed in favour of continued move-ment north. The 39th Infantry from the 9th Division assumed responsibility for reducing and occupying coastal strongpoints and inland batteries on 12 June. Early that morning the 2/39th Infantry approached Crisbecq and found the Germans had abandoned the position during the night[51] leaving behind some of their wounded and American prisoners.

By the end of the first week in Normandy, the Americans established a unified beachhead through the capture of coastal towns and Carentan on the River Douve. The 101st linked up with infantry from the Omaha area. The 82nd Airborne secured a bridgehead across the Merderet and would soon participate in the movement westwards across the base of the Cotentin to the Atlantic coast. Infantry divisions in the VII Corps were poised to continue their drive up the peninsula to the port of Cherbourg. They also entered and participated in the destruction of Norman towns, experienced their first encounters with the civilian population and seized increasing numbers of Wehrmacht prisoners from Germany and various conquered regions of Europe.

(**Opposite, above**) A medical unit carrying stretchers lands at Les Dunes de Madeleine on D-Day as photographed by Shelton. (*NARA*)

(**Opposite, below**) Shelton recorded an infantry unit advancing from Utah Beach. The date was listed as 9 June and the unit as the 8th Infantry of the 4th Division. Since Shelton recorded photographs at a field hospital on 9 June, the date may be inaccurate. In addition, the circular shoulder patch design looks more like that of the 9th Division. (*NARA*)

(**Opposite, above**) Franklin photographed an artillery shell explosion on the beach in an image dated 11 June but possibly on D-Day. (*NARA*)

(**Opposite, below**) A group from the 2nd Ranger Battalion including a .30 calibre machine gun on D-Day or early in the Normandy invasion. The scene has been attributed to Pointe du Hoc but the 2nd Battalion also landed at Omaha Beach. The image is one of the few to show troops in combat conditions. (*NARA*)

(**Above**) Soldiers and prisoners at Pointe du Hoc on 12 June as recorded by photographer Lovelle (or Lavelle). (*NARA*)

A view of Red Beach sector at Utah Beach on 8 June recorded by Petrony. (*NARA*)

An abandoned German 47mm PAK anti-tank gun blocked a narrow gap at Les Dunes de Madeleine in the photograph on 12 June by Kaye. (*NARA*)

A Sherman tank drives off an LST probably onto Utah Beach on 9 June. Intake and exhaust vents have been fitted in case the tank had been launched at sea to 'swim' for shore. (NARA)

Shelton photographed soldiers of the 8th Infantry, 4th Division marching through a coastal wetland on the Cotentin Peninsula on 9 June. (NARA)

(**Above**) The battery at Crisbecq on a headland north of Saint-Marcouf was among the most formidable on the east coast of the Cotentin. The position contained casemates mounting 210mm guns with underground ammunition storage and connected communication trenches. The 2nd Battalion of the 22nd Infantry advanced on the nearby battery at Azeville while the 1st Battalion moved through the village of Saint-Marcouf to attack Crisbecq on 7 June. Both attacks were repulsed (Ruppenthal, *Utah Beach to Cherbourg*, pp. 66–8). Trichka photographed the Crisbecq position on 2 August. *(NARA)*

(**Opposite, above**) Dutro photographed an American leaning over a casualty – possibly a German – near a burning casemate on 9 June. The casemate had sustained damage from American fire. The 22nd Infantry of the 4th Division advanced northwards along the coast to capture enemy defence positions. However, the 3/22nd also moved against the battery position at Azeville on that day. The troops directed bazooka and tank fire on a concrete blockhouse, then used satchel charges, all of which proved ineffective. Ultimately Private Ralph Riley used a flame thrower to ignite ammunition inside the blockhouse, leading to the surrender of this position and the entire battery (Ruppenthal, *Utah Beach to Cherbourg*, pp. 105 and 107). *(NARA)*

(**Opposite, below**) Soldiers of the 9th Division on the march through Saint-Marie-du-Mont inland from Utah Beach as photographed by Zwick on 13 June. *(NARA)*

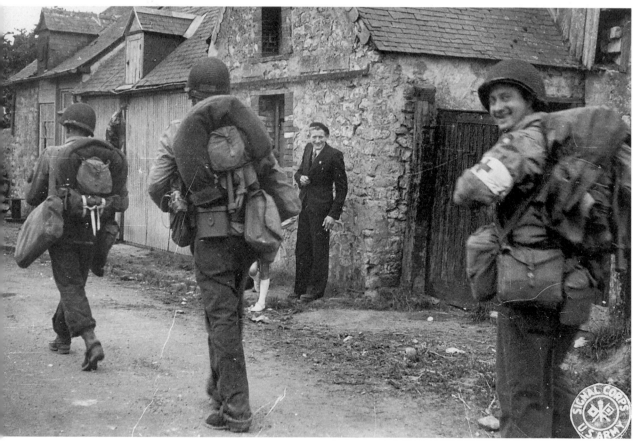

# Chapter Seven

# Soldiers, Prisoners and Civilians

### The 502nd Parachute Infantry in Saint-Marcouf

Detachment J of the 165th Signal Photographic Company – the company of Herman Wall and Richard Taylor – was assigned to the 101st Airborne and Werner was evidently one of the photographers. He accompanied a 101st unit into the small village of Saint-Marcouf on 8 June and recorded one of the most remarkable sequences of early interactions between soldiers and civilians.

As mentioned in the previous chapter, Saint-Marcouf was located north of Utah Beach near large German gun emplacements and thus was an area of intense interest as the Americans extended their beachhead northwards up the Cotentin Peninsula. A battalion of the 22nd Infantry entered the village on successive days (7 and 8 June) during unsuccessful attempts to capture the nearby guns at Crisbecq.[52]

Paratroopers accompanied the infantry on the 8th of June. The unit was probably from the 1/502nd that had fought to stabilize the northern flank on D-Day with their commander Lieutenant Colonel Patrick Cassidy. The numbers of troops in some of the photographs suggest a full platoon, but the presence of a captain may indicate that all of the members of his company who had appeared by that time participated. The specific company remains a mystery since 502nd unit records indicate the 1st Battalion was relieved by the 4th Division on the morning of 7 June and moved southwards from the area with the remainder of the regiment.

Carell noted that German troops from the Crisbecq battery had captured twenty paratroopers from a company headquarters in the 502nd Parachute Infantry who landed near the battery and village north of their drop zone. Captured parachutists were often freed on D-Day and the following days as the Americans advanced north.

The rubble visible in some photographs reflects pre-invasion bombing or subsequent shelling on 7 June. During the evening of 5–6 June Allied bombers had sought to eliminate the nearby heavy gun batteries. Carell reported the bombing lasted about thirty-five minutes.[53] While the battery at Crisbecq was the target, some of the bombs fell on nearby villages. The tower and roof of the Saint-Marcouf church were destroyed and thirty-six residents were killed, including six members of the Carré-Creully family who were buried in the churchyard.

## African American Soldiers in Normandy

Photographs by Todd show African American soldiers armed and on a combat patrol. The group may have been associated with an artillery unit; another photograph shows such a unit with the slogan 'From Harlem to Hitler' painted on the barrel of a 105mm howitzer. Black soldiers served for the most part in construction and transportation units in Normandy such as the truck drivers of 'Red Ball Express' that was the principal means of moving supplies from the beaches inland, at ever greater distances.

Diaries of the period contain comments that are not flattering and at times racist. In the segregated US Army of the 1940s, African American soldiers were generally not welcomed by many white soldiers. Instructions not to take black prisoners were issued within certain battalions in the 1st SS Panzer and 17th SS Panzergrenadier Divisions in Normandy. Murders of French black colonial troops had occurred earlier during the rapid advance of the Wehrmacht in 1940.[54]

American black soldiers came to France with ideas that residents in the country and particularly in Paris were less prejudiced and therefore more willing to fraternize with them. This was at times the case. In one village, local residents had come to know and respect black GIs rather than white soldiers whom they regarded as frequently drunk and filled with hatred.[55] However, prejudice placed the African Americans at risk from both American military police and the local population. Black soldiers were accused of sexual assaults more frequently than were their white counterparts. In France, thirty-four soldiers were executed for violent crimes against civilians and refugees; of the twenty-one executed for rape, eighteen were black and only three were white; sentences were reduced to imprisonment for twenty-one other black soldiers. African American soldiers were only about 10 per cent of the American Army in France.[56] Roberts argued the high incidence of charges against African Americans possibly reflected a particular prejudice against black troops among civilians in rural France. She stridently contended that the deep prejudice in the American Army of the period made authorities more inclined to suspect and accuse black soldiers, who were often arrested simply for being in the vicinity at the time crimes were committed. When French stories of and outrage against sexual violence suffered by civilians spread to the newspapers in Cherbourg in the fall of 1944, she suggested American military authorities blamed the minority black soldiers to a disproportionate degree as a means of salvaging the honour of their army.[57]

## Prisoners

Early images from the invasion reveal troops that appear happy to have surrendered and thus stood a much greater chance of surviving the war. One of the striking images that emerges is the contrast in ages among the soldiers and presence of boys and very young men. The cost of nearly five years of war required the Third Reich to obtain soldiers from numerous occupied countries and to place them in regiments and battalions of questionable dedication to the tasks at hand. The other issue was age, since increasing use was made of youth and older men.

Military formations of varying quality constituted the German Army in France. Troops ranged from coastal divisions such as 716th and 243rd considered to be lower grade, often with attached battalions from conquered lands to the east, through seasoned infantry divisions of good quality such as 352nd to the armoured units that were held back from the beaches. The latter were often Waffen-SS units with much younger soldiers than the others.

Data from a December 1943 roster reveal the stark contrasts. The 243rd Division consisted mostly of older men, with nearly two-thirds of its soldiers between 31 and 38 years of age and some even older. The 21st Panzer Division, rebuilt after its loss in Tunisia, had a more even distribution, with 40 per cent being 22–30 years old. Nearly two-thirds of the 9th and 10th SS Panzer Divisions were less than 21 years of age; both returned from Russia in late June to fight in Normandy. The 12th SS Panzer Division *Hitlerjugend* was the ultimate in youthful vigour with more than 85 per cent of its soldiers being 20 years old or less.[58]

Most of the SS units opposed the British and Canadians in the eastern sector. The Americans were confronted in June and July by the 17th SS Panzer Grenadier Division (motorized infantry with a battalion of assault guns for support) and the 2nd SS Panzer Division, the latter having marched up from south-western France leaving destruction and civilian murder in its wake.

The act of surrender was fraught with danger and there are numerous examples of soldiers on both sides refusing to accept the surrender of their enemies, as discussed by Ellis and Kennett. Civilians were of course a different matter. Leleu suggested killings in the West were less reflections of racial ideology than a desire to justify an elite military status. He argued there was no comparison between the actions of the 10th SS Panzer Division that spent twenty months in the West with 'only' several summary executions, and the earlier experience of the *Totenkopf* (Death's Head) Division that within ten days killed hundreds of civilians and prisoners of war in the north of France in May 1940. On balance, Leleu held that instances of 'war crimes' by Waffen-SS troops in Normandy were not greatly distinguished from those by other Wehrmacht troops or indeed by the Allies, with one exception: the 12th SS Panzer Division.[59] The division had massacred eighty-six civilians in Ascq in the north of France in April 1944. They had executed no less than 178 Allied prisoners (mostly Canadian) and several dozen civilians in Normandy; 156 of the Allied prisoners were killed during the first two weeks of the invasion, amounting to one of every three soldiers captured by the division during the first week.

The 2nd SS Panzer Division *Das Reich* had perpetrated horrific crimes against civilian populations in Tulle and in Oradour in 1944; this division had been schooled in the racial war practised in the East and brought those practices to France. The youthful soldiers in the 12th SS had yet to engage in combat, so the explanation for their behaviour lay elsewhere, perhaps in the particular indoctrination received in the Hitler Youth. Such behaviour was complicated by the fact that a senior staff officer in the division had clearly ordered that as many prisoners as possible be captured. However, certain regimental commanders did not hesitate to transgress the rules or norms of warfare, at least as practised in the West.[60]

## Civilians

The American Army began the invasion of Europe in 1944 with many preconceptions about the French, most of which were dispelled. Those who had some schoolboy French language usually found it of almost no help. They were confused by language difficulties and social norms of behaviour, some of which were generally French and others peculiar to the rural province of Normandy.

While very grateful for the arrival of the Allies and the liberation that followed, the local population at times found the behaviour of those liberators confusing. By early July the US VIII Corps addressed instances of looting, property destruction and robbery of civilians by American forces. The memorandum observed 'such conduct prejudices our relations with the civilian population who willingly and even cheerfully accept the destruction of property that is the result of our military action but cannot understand vandalism practised by certain of our soldiers.'[61]

Preconceptions were of course not confined to the liberators. The material abundance of the Allies and especially the Americans meant access to foods which Norman residents had never encountered or rarely seen since 1940. Some farm families in Normandy ate the high quality food scraps given to them for farm animals by American mess officers.[62] Henry Ferri was deeply affected by what he saw. He commented many years later that when he witnessed children and older people starving or observed some women prepared to sell themselves for cigarettes, he came away with a strong desire to help his fellow man. After the war he returned to America and became a teacher.

Such scenes were as troubling to the French as to the Allies. Many French men felt a deep sense of humiliation at the collapse of their army's eastern and northern fronts in 1940 and the resulting occupation of the country. The behaviour of women in the country – sometimes real, more often imagined – reinforced this sense of shame. Spectacles where men shaved the hair from women accused of collaboration with German soldiers provided a means of directing this shame against a portion of their own population whom paradoxically they had failed to protect. Many American soldiers were appalled at such public abuse of women, which lowered their regard for the French involved.

French society was also concerned about the reputation the country was acquiring for begging food and favours from the Allies. The frequent appearance of children asking for food and cigarettes and attention paid to the soldiers by some young women proved embarrassing to a broad spectrum of the French population.[63] Newspapers and community leaders argued that a return of social order and decorum was required to restore French honour. Anthony Eden, British Foreign Secretary and First World War veteran, summarized the complex emotions within a recently liberated country when he observed those who had not suffered through an occupation could not judge the behaviour of citizens in countries that had been occupied.[64]

(**Above**) A photograph by Werner dated 6 June, but possibly recorded prior to departure of the patrol or in Saint-Marcouf on 8 June. The officer standing at right is the same captain shown on page 124. *(NARA)*

(**Opposite, above**) The patrol from the 502nd entering Saint-Marcouf. The members of this squad were marching separately in case of ambush. *(NARA)*

(**Opposite, below**) A machine-gun crew in the fields and on the road near the town. They are not wearing airborne slacks or boots and may be infantry from the 4th Division. *(NARA)*

(**Above**) A squad marching along the street adjacent to the church. One soldier was watching the rear with a tense expression. The soldier at right has a bayonet fixed to his rifle. The photo does not show any of the damage sustained by the church on the night of 5–6 June. (*NARA*) (**Below**) The same view in September 2014.

(**Above**) The squad has advanced to the lower end of the street. This is a curious photograph and may have been staged. While some troopers were seeking the shelter of the embankment at right, the smiling figure in the street had been tensely guarding the rear a few moments earlier. The sergeant rested on masonry rubble from the bombing on the night of 5–6 June. (*NARA*) (**Below**) The same view in September 2014.

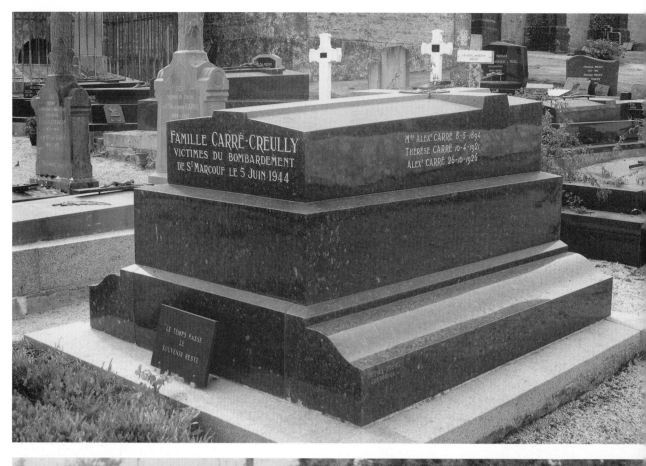

FAMILLE CARRÉ-CREULLY
VICTIMES DU BOMBARDEMENT
DE St MARCOUF LE 5 JUIN 1944

Mme ALEXe CARRÉ 8-5-1894
THÉRÈSE CARRÉ 10-4-1921
ALEXe CARRÉ 26-10-1926

LE TEMPS PASSE
LE
SOUVENIR RESTE

(**Opposite, above**) The tomb of a family of six, among the thirty-six civilian victims of the Allied bombing on the night of 5–6 June.

(**Opposite, below**) This sergeant passed a French woman as he entered Saint-Marcouf. Her dazed expression perhaps reflected bewilderment following the bombing and subsequent events of the past two days near her village. (*NARA*)

(**Above**) Another encounter between members of the patrol and a French citizen on the outskirts of town. The sergeant in the foreground may be the same as in the above photograph with the woman. The full packs, map cases and ammunition pouches were common equipment. A film of this same scene reveals the citizen limping as he approached the soldiers. (*NARA*)

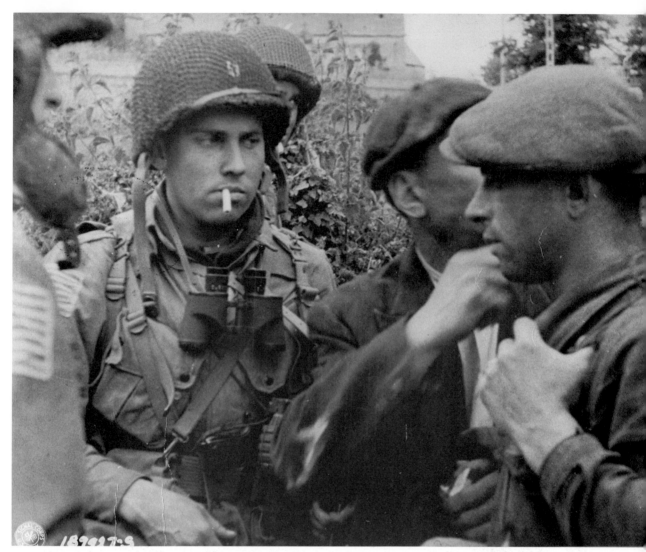

(**Above**) The captain seen in the initial photograph has encountered two local men who were probably members of the Resistance. His suspicious gaze might reflect language difficulties or uncertainty of the tactical situation. The village church is visible in the background. (*NARA*)

(**Opposite, above**) A friendly encounter with local residents. For many children in Normandy, the Americans were a source of chocolate, candy and endless fascination. (*NARA*)

(**Opposite, below**) The patrol members in Saint-Marcouf, appearing more relaxed. The mixed nature of the group is indicated by helmet stencils reflecting the 501st (diamond) and divisional artillery (circle or cannonball). A possible spade symbol for the 506th is partially visible. There is no 502nd stencil (heart) indicated in this photograph, although one may be visible on page 121 (top). Such heart-shaped symbols are clearly seen on page 34 (top). (*NARA*)

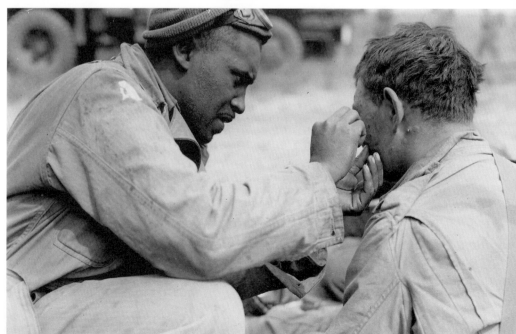

(**Opposite, above**) A rifle squad with a captured Nazi flag, one of the prized items sought by troops. A German helmet with a pencilled inscription was also shown in the foreground. The youth of many of the troopers was readily apparent. Normandy was the initiation to combat for the 101st Airborne. (*NARA*)

(**Opposite, below**) Army photographer Todd recorded scenes on and near the Omaha beachhead during the first week of the invasion. The presence of African American soldiers may have been especially interesting to him. 'By picking a small bit of metal from his face, an American Negro soldier lends a hand to another American. Scenes like this were common on the Beachheads in Northern France where American troops rolled onto the Continent in vast numbers.' [Original caption to Todd photograph on 8 June.] The goggles on the soldier at left suggest the men were welders. (*NARA*)

(**Above**) A patrol of African American soldiers – possibly from an artillery unit – with an officer in the centre enter a farmyard in Vierville. They are passing the lean-to shed at the end of the barn seen in the following image. [Todd photograph on 10 June.] (*NARA*)

(**Above**) The same patrol moved to the front of the barn and encountered or was accompanied by a group of white soldiers in the farmyard. Their officer was descending a ladder near the commander of the other group. The soldier with the clip pouch on the rear of his web belt appeared in both photographs. The African American soldiers were armed with M1 carbines and M1903 bolt action rifles. [Photograph on 10 June probably by Todd.] *(NARA)*

(**Opposite, above**) Battery A of the 333th Field Artillery Battalion fires its 155mm guns in support of the 90th Division near Périers during Operation Cobra on 28 July as photographed by Rothenberger. *(NARA)*

(**Opposite, below**) Prisoners from Georgia serving in the German army whose prospects for survival have increased dramatically, photographed on 8 June. However, all those who returned to the Soviet Union from the west were treated with suspicion or worse, and those who had served in the German army or had been prisoners in Germany were even more suspect. *(NARA)*

Himes recorded this image of prisoners of varying ages under British guard on 8 June. The prisoner with possessions on a stick was less than 18 years old and another seems even younger. (*NARA*)

These soldiers must have been considered sufficiently trustworthy to be allowed knives with their rations. Todd recorded the image on 9 June, which provides an especially good view of the hobnailed boots provided to Wehrmacht soldiers. (*NARA*)

German soldiers cross a ridge with hands raised in surrender on 9 June. An American officer is crouching at the right edge of the image. (*NARA*)

A contrast between two other prisoners also in England: a youthful sailor and older soldier. The age range among Germans who defended Normandy was striking. The photograph was recorded by Jones on 11 June. (*NARA*)

(**Opposite, above**) Prisoners marching along a beach, likely Utah, on 8 June. (*NARA*)

(**Opposite, below**) A German soldier who was partially buried when a trench collapsed due to artillery shelling was photographed by Dutro on the Cotentin on 9 June. The caption indicated he shortly became a prisoner. (*NARA*)

(**Above**) A column of German prisoners near the town of Saint-Jean-de-Daye photographed by Locell on 11 July. (*NARA*)

Wilkes photographed a German prisoner on 15 July who had been treated by American medics. *(NARA)*

A German position is surrendered near Saint-Lô on 20 July as photographed by Witscher. The town had been entered and occupied on the previous day after weeks of fighting. (NARA)

Spangle recorded an image of a German Luftwaffe prisoner being brought in for questioning on 26 July. (NARA)

(**Opposite, above**) The 4th Armoured Division accepted the surrender of Germans in Coutances during the Cobra advance. Ornitz photographed the scene on 29 July. (*NARA*)

(**Opposite, below**) Encounter on 7 June photographed by Schultz between a local farmer and members of the 29th Division including a private as interpreter. (*NARA*)

(**Above**) Lavelle recorded Rangers and three generations of a family moving along a Norman village street on either the 7th or 13th of June. The family was apparently seeking milk or water. (*NARA*)

(**Above**) Private Roland Bonnell (left) and Sergeant James Devine with a small girl and her puppy photographed by Fougel on 13 June in Colleville-sur-Mer. (*NARA*)

(**Opposite, above**) Witscher photographed an 82nd Airborne paratrooper carrying luggage for an apparently cheerful family in Sainte-Mère-Église on 8 June. Items included bedding, clothing and coat hangers. On the evening of D-Day, no relief from the sea had arrived in town and rumours were circulating the landings had not taken place. The mayor overheard some women pleading with the Americans not to leave them. One paratrooper smiled and said, 'we will never leave you, we will die on this spot.' (Maire de Sainte-Mère-Église letter, 505th Parachute Infantry records). (*NARA*)

(**Opposite, below**) A classic image by Weintraub of Americans passing cheering French civilians on a narrow village street on 13 June. The half-track vehicle is towing a cart or artillery piece. (*NARA*)

(**Above**) A French family shares wine and champagne – presumably stored with care during the occupation – with an American infantry officer. The farmer seems unimpressed with the bottle of Bordeaux in his hand. Weintraub photographed this scene on the same day, 13 June. *(NARA)*

(**Opposite, above**) A grittier image of the impact of war: a family salvages what remains in the ruins of their home in Normandy on 15 June in a photograph by Bowen. *(NARA)*

(**Opposite, below**) Corporal Buster Sanchez from Louisiana distributes bread abandoned by the Germans to citizens in Notre Dame de Cenilly. Some of the ambivalence and shame forced upon a proud population by hunger is apparent. *(NARA)*

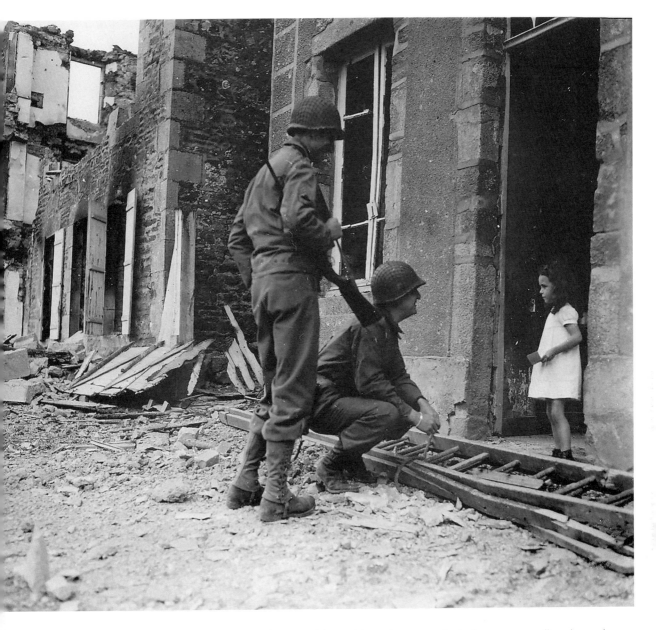

(**Opposite, above**) Bastille Day 1944 (14 July) was celebrated in various ways including men parading shamed *collaboratrices* through the streets of Cherbourg. Kaye photographed the scene. (*NARA*)

(**Opposite, below**) Private Irving Scott of Croton-on-Hudson, New York, a medic with Company I, 134th Infantry of the 35th Division, provides aid to injured children. Caliendo photographed the scene on 15 July. (*NARA*)

(**Above**) Root photographed two soldiers greeting one of the last residents of Cerisy on 25 July. (*NARA*)

A refugee family including a nursing mother and injured older woman – possibly her mother – near Saint-Lô in late July. (NARA)

Salvas photographed a group of refugees huddled in Saint-Lô on 26 July roughly one week after the town fell to the Americans. (NARA)

Older women who had seen much during their lives were still present to be photographed by Caliendo on 29 July. (NARA)

# Chapter Eight

# Advance to Cherbourg and Interior to Saint-Lô

Inland movement from the American beachheads had the initial goal of linking those areas, with emphasis westwards from Omaha to secure the coastal towns of Grandcamp and Isigny by the 29th Division (mostly the 116th Infantry) supported by armoured forces. Eventually those forces would move along the Vire and Douve estuaries to establish contact with troops from the Cotentin Peninsula at Carentan. The American divisions that initially landed at Omaha Beach also moved southwards and inland. The 1st Division was charged with maintaining contact on the eastern flank with British troops that had landed on Gold Beach.

The 29th Division advanced southwards and became embroiled in two unfortunate incidents involving the 115th Infantry. The first was a night 'ambush' early on 10 June near Lison and Carrefour on 2/115th. German infantry and armour that had been bypassed was falling back during the night of 9–10 June when it stumbled onto the 2/115th that had not taken a strong defensive position. In the ensuing melee, at least two German tanks were disabled but the entire 2nd Battalion was disorganized and dispersed. The battalion commander Lieutenant Colonel William Warfield was among the dead found in the morning. The 3/115th also undertook an unsuccessful attempt to cross the River Elle and secure a bridgehead on 12 June.[65]

From the outset, advances to establish a linkage between bridgeheads or sustain movement inland towards Saint-Lô were conducted with simultaneous movements to isolate the Cotentin Peninsula and seize the important port of Cherbourg. The infantry divisions landed on Utah Beach were the major forces charged with the movement up the peninsula: the 4th, 9th, 79th and 90th. Movement across the peninsula was undertaken by the 82nd Airborne that included the capture of Saint-Sauveur, the location that had been the division's objective in an earlier airborne plan.

Difficulty of movement through the *bocage* landscape of thick hedgerows bordering fields of irregular sizes was the predominant memory of most soldiers who advanced through that country. John Cotter, an infantryman in the 90th Division, remembered moving into such a field on the Cotentin carrying a BAR in a rifle squad. He noticed one soldier on the flank positioned within a hedgerow. Cotter thought

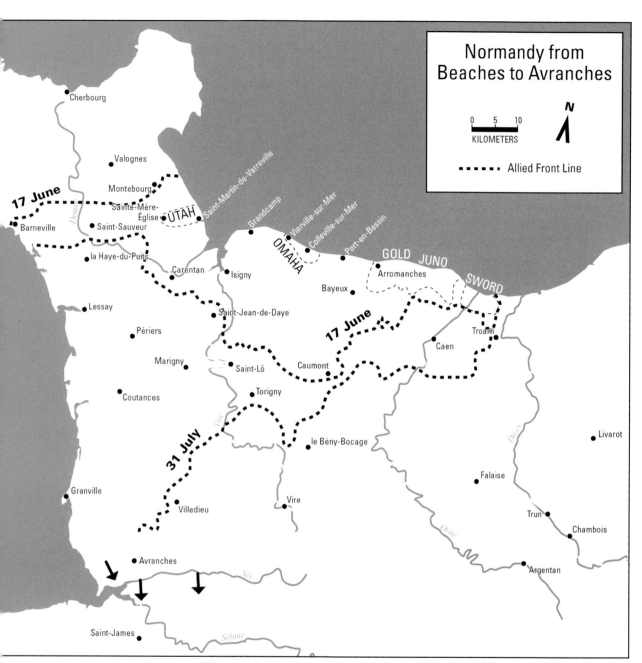

Normandy from Beaches to Avranches.

that man fortunate until a German mortar barrage swept through their position. The enemy knew such hedgerows would be attractive to advancing infantry. As the sergeant ordered the men to fall back, Cotter turned and saw only a smoking hole where the soldier on the flank had sought protection.

Most American infantry would advance until they encountered a hedgerow defended by Germans entrenched in a ditch behind the hedge. The Americans would often occupy a ditch behind the nearest hedgerow and exchange fire until artillery or armoured support compelled the enemy to retire. The 505th Parachute Infantry adopted a more aggressive tactical approach. A platoon would divide into two groups and move forward along the hedges at each edge of the field. If the field presented a lateral edge of 75 metres or so, the groups would move forward on the outside of the flank hedges. If the lateral edge was longer – say 200 metres or so – movement was up the inside. A column would inevitably draw fire that was returned by the riflemen. A soldier with a portable automatic weapon such as a BAR or Thompson sub-machine gun would crawl forward as far as possible, then sweep the opposing hedgerow. A second soldier with an automatic weapon from further back in the column would be covered by as much gunfire as could be brought to bear, including mortars. The second soldier would attempt to crawl all the way forward into the edge of the opposing hedgerow. If successful, he would be on the flank of the enemy trench and could devastate that position with automatic fire. The success of the tactic was attributed to 'heavy, penetrating automatic fire on the enemy, but more so to the aggressiveness and willingness of the individual soldier to advance under fire'.[66]

By midday on 16 June Lieutenant Colonel Vandervoort stood overlooking Saint-Sauveur: 'From where I am standing I can see everything – the town is full of Germans – our artillery is in a position to really give them Hell, I tell you Norton, this is it! This is the place to really cut off the Krauts and cut off the peninsula. If we don't take advantage of this, we are crazy – and I'm counting on you to get this information back to Colonel Ekman and General Ridgway. Tell them to come up here and see for themselves.' The regiment moved forward to occupy the town that had been and was still being attacked by the Air Corps. It was subsequently reported the Germans had evacuated much of the territory between Saint-Sauveur and the sea. The nearly constant action of course exacted a toll: by 27 June it was reported that the effective strength of the 505th had been reduced to 42 per cent of the officers and 50 per cent of the enlisted men who had jumped into Normandy in the early hours of 6 June.[67]

This was also the case as the divisions advanced north towards Cherbourg and the end of the Cherbourg Peninsula. The German troops that had been stationed on the peninsula since the invasion continued to resist and placed increasing faith in the fortified points within the city. The Americans were mystified at the decision by the Germans to fall back from positions on ridges to the south of the city.[68] Still, resistance was strong and did not end even with the surrender of the garrison commander General Karl-Wilhelm von Schlieben. By the time the city had fallen into American hands, demolitions along the harbour front had rendered the port unusable for months. The vast majority of supplies to sustain the Allied forces in Normandy would continue to move inland across the invasion beaches.

The advance southwards towards Saint-Lô was even more costly. The 29th and other divisions had made little progress through the *bocage* during June and early July. Unit commanders were encouraged, chastised and replaced. German defenders used the terrain to maximum advantage. Movement of less than a mile would be obtained at the cost of hundreds of casualties in the battalions and regiments involved. As discussed in Chapter Nine, rates of combat exhaustion began to rise in the divisions.

The costs were also high for the Germans and the occupation of points such as Hill 122 north of town on 15 July by the 35th Division deprived the defenders of much-needed artillery observation. Ultimately pressure became too great and the depleted German divisions fell back through the ruins of Saint-Lô. After weeks of dogged advance, the 29th Division organized a task force of infantry and armour led by their reconnaissance troop and entered the eastern end of the town on 18 July.[69]

The German forces in Normandy for the most part enjoyed their postings in France, certainly in comparison with alternatives in Italy, the Balkans and the Eastern Front. Once the invasion began, the reality of war quickly enveloped them. Some of their weapons such as light machine guns, anti-tank rockets and multiple barrel mortars or *Nebelwerfer* were superior to those of the Allied forces. The quality of their tanks, particularly the Mark V Panthers and Mark VI Tigers, exceeded Cromwell and Sherman tanks both in terms of armoured protection and the penetrating power of their guns.[70] Several Shermans were lost for every German tank destroyed.[71] While not an American effort, the experience of the Irish Guards in north-west Europe reflected the broader Allied predicament. They understood that virtually any German tank – including the smaller Mark IV – was capable of destroying the Sherman while among the latter only those mounting the British 17 pounder gun were consistently effective in opposition.

The 2nd Battalion Irish Guards arrived in Normandy in July with sixty-one tanks. Only two were still in operation at the end of the war; both of these had been twice put out of action and repaired. The Sherman tanks with their gasoline engines frequently burned when struck by the German 75mm or the vaunted 88mm guns. However, the Shermans that became the mainstay of the Allied armies in Europe had an enviable record for mechanical reliability and were available in sufficient quantities to replace battle losses. As Bradley noted, this frequency of replacement offered little comfort to the crews.[72]

As the battles in Normandy developed, the hedgerows and the German tanks and anti-tank weapons proved important elements in stymying attempts to advance. German infantry and artillery were clearly crucial to the defence. However, Allied naval vessels provided powerful artillery support near the coast not only on D-Day but during the initial weeks of the campaign. Allied air forces were increasingly relied upon to rout out enemy forces and particularly to attack tanks and vehicle columns from the air. German vehicles were usually covered with bushes and must have resembled moving hedges, while infantry frequently looked skyward.

The Allied commanders convinced their air marshals to employ medium and heavy bombers to attack front line positions in preparation for assaults by infantry and armour on both the American and British/Canadian fronts. The start line for the American assault in late July was formed along the road between Périers and Saint-Lô. Infantry from several divisions with armoured support were assembled behind the road and were prepared to advance following the devastating release of thousands of pounds of high explosive bombs on the enemy front line.

The architect of American strategy for use of armour – and thus a direct influence on the design of that armour – was Lesley McNair. Since he believed tanks would be used to exploit breakouts into the enemy rear and not to fight other tanks, he was evidently eager to witness the beginning of such a breakout. Operation Cobra offered such an opportunity. When the heavy bombers came over to pound the enemy front line, they flew across the American lines and some loads fell among the waiting infantry, killing more than a hundred soldiers in the 9th and 30th Divisions. There was no little irony that General McNair was among those killed.

The breakout during Operation Cobra was ultimately a success. American troops that had been struggling to advance through a few miles or less of fields and hedge-rows began to realize that the German defence line was crumbling. By 1 August, the American Third Army under General George Patton became operational. Once the motorized divisions passed through the narrow neck of land near Avranches, they began to advance west into Brittany, south to the River Loire and eastwards to begin a grand encirclement of the remaining German forces in Normandy.

A German counter-offensive sought to cut the American lines near Avranches. The Allies had advance warning of the effort through intercepts from Enigma code messages. The 30th Division was isolated for a time on a hilltop near Mortain. Nevertheless, German efforts to drive west to the coast resulted in a bizarre pattern of movement more deeply into encircling Allied forces driving east. The British and Canadians continued to move southwards from Caen to exert pressure on the German front.

American troops reached Argentan on 13 August but halted rather than con-tinuing an encircling movement northwards to Falaise. Despite protests from Patton, Bradley decided to hold a strong position near Argentan since he thought his available forces were insufficient to stem the desperate German retreat. Patton then began an advance to the Seine.

Canadian troops reached Falaise on 17 August and extended some elements south to the village of Saint-Lambert-sur-Dives. The Polish 1st Armoured Division pushed down to Chambois on 19 August to meet the American 90th Division moving up from the south. Other elements of the Polish division were posted on high ground overlooking the German retreat route. They held their heights despite repeated efforts of the Germans to dislodge them. In the end, thousands of German infantry were killed or surrendered, although rather more escaped to the east through a narrow route that remained open. Most of their armoured vehicles and other means of transport remained within the Falaise Pocket.

By the evening of 24 August the first elements the French *2e Division blindée* commanded by General Jacques-Philippe Leclerc had arrived in Paris. The city was liberated the next day when the remainder of Leclerc's 2nd Armoured Division entered. Support was provided by a regiment from the American 4th Division. Given the casualties sustained by that division since landing at Utah Beach, it seems likely that many of those who entered Paris had arrived in Normandy as replacements after D-Day.

By 1 September the Allied armies were driving rapidly towards Belgium or into eastern France. Soldiers, ammunition, vehicles and supplies continued to flow across the beaches, although it was necessary to move them increasingly greater distances to keep pace with the advancing armies. Behind them lay devastated towns and destroyed bridges that would take years to repair. Civilian losses would never be forgotten. Many soldiers remained for a time in Normandy, having been wounded in the first three months of the campaign. Thousands of soldiers – Allied and German – would never leave.

Massenge recorded an anti-tank gun firing on a German position in 'Fort de Fougaville' on 10 June. (*NARA*)

(**Above**) The ruined town of Isigny between Omaha Beach and the Cotentin on 13 June. (*NARA*)

(**Opposite, above**) A view of Bérigny by Moran on 20 June. The crossroads en route to Saint-Lô was considered an ideal position for German defence. Artillery or bomb impact holes were visible in the fields. (*NARA*)

(**Opposite, below**) An aerial view of Cherbourg harbor on 21 June. The various harbour breakwaters were defended by stone fortifications from another era. (*NARA*)

Two soldiers throwing grenades over a garden wall in Cherbourg. (*NARA*)

(**Opposite, above**) Soldiers with a grenade launcher during the advance into Cherbourg. (*NARA*)

(**Opposite, below**) 79th Division soldiers advancing along the Rue de Paris near the public gardens in Cherbourg (Benamou, *Normandy 1944*, p. 106) on 27 June. (*NARA*)

(**Opposite, above**) American commanders observe smoke reflecting German demolitions along the waterfront in Cherbourg. Petrony photographed the group on 27 June. (*NARA*)

(**Opposite, below**) General Joe Collins and Mayor Paul Renaud celebrate the liberation of Cherbourg, as photographed by Zwick on 28 June. (*NARA*)

(**Above, left**) A vegetable market has opened in the city near a 'Teinturerie' or wall hanging shop. (*NARA*)

(**Above, right**) The family in a small stone house proudly displayed the tricolor. They were fortunate to have a home that remained standing. (*NARA*)

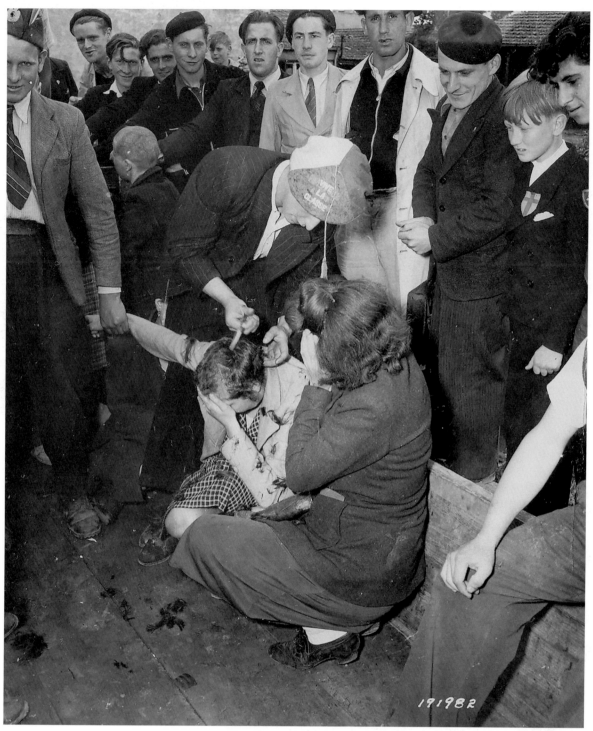

The darker side of the Bastille Day 1944 celebration in Cherbourg, probably photographed by Kaye. A woman has her hair cut off – the punishment for those who collaborated with the Germans – in front of a crowd of men and boys. Another woman awaits a similar punishment, while a previous victim is visible in the background. (NARA)

The joint Franco-American parade recorded by La Franco on 14 or 15 July. *(NARA)*

A June 1944 photograph by Wagner of one of the more formidable German anti-tank weapons, the *Jagdpanther*. The vehicle used the Panther chassis but lacked a rotating turret and gearing. It was therefore lighter in weight, but carried the powerful 88mm gun. The sloping frontal profile served to deflect tank and artillery shells and increased the protection offered by its armour. This vehicle may be moving forward to confront the British or Canadians. The photograph may on the other hand predate the invasion since no camouflage was present. *(Bundesarchiv)*

Theobald may have staged this photograph during a meal break for Wehrmacht infantry during the summer of 1944 but the possibility of air attack was a reality for all German forces in Normandy.
(*Bundesarchiv*)

(**Opposite, above**) This German armoured personnel carrier, the equivalent of the American half-track, shows the increasingly typical brushwork covering used by vehicles for protection from air attack. The Allies benefited from almost total air superiority in Normandy. Theobald photographed the vehicle moving in June 1944. (*Bundesarchiv*)

(**Opposite, below**) Pilots study a Panther tank that has been put out of action in a photograph taken on 19 July. The image also provides a good view of a narrow lane bordered by hedges common on the Normandy landscape. (*NARA*)

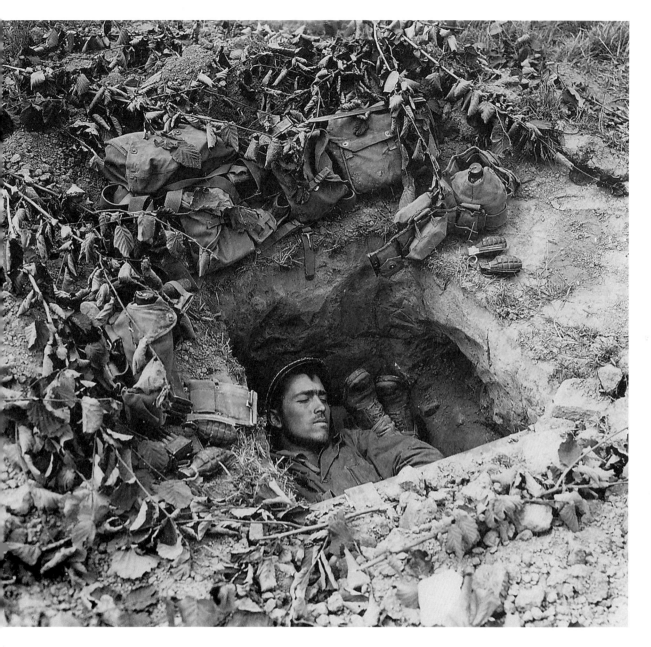

(**Opposite, above**) German infantry use the cover provided by stone farm buildings possibly on the outskirts of Saint-Lô to oppose the American advance. Reich photographed the scene in the summer of 1944. (*Bundesarchiv*)

(**Opposite, below**) An observer from the 1/137th Infantry of the 35th Division sheltered behind a hedgerow as photographed by Musae on 11 July. (*NARA*)

(**Above**) A pair of soldiers seeking protection in a narrow slit trench while sleeping on 11 July photographed by Collier. (*NARA*)

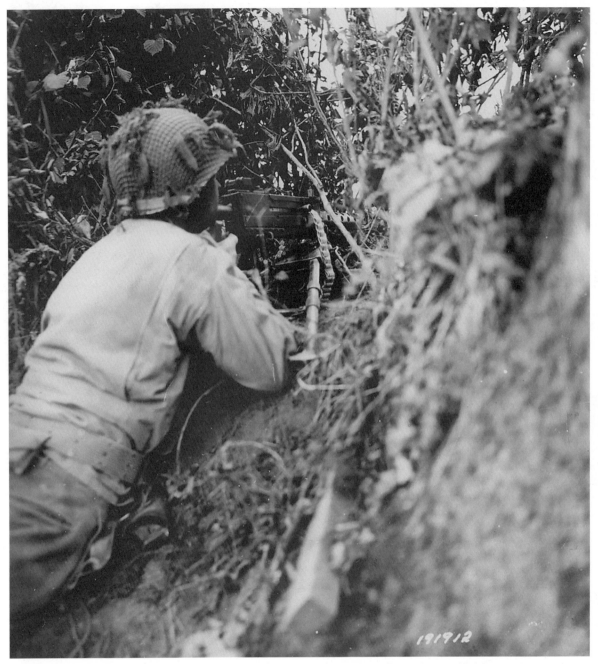

(**Above**) A machine-gun post in defilade provided by the thick growth of a hedge on 15 July. (*NARA*)

(**Opposite, above**) Carolan photographed the 175th Infantry of the 29th Division on 15 July digging in along one of the hedgerows north-east of Saint-Lô during their slow advance. (*NARA*)

(**Opposite, below**) Medics from the 320th Infantry of the 35th Division assist a German wounded by a grenade on Hill 97 north of Saint-Lô. (*NARA*)

191668

(**Above**) Infantry from the 35th Division occupied Hill 122 north of Saint-Lô on 15 July and eliminated the artillery observation points that hampered the advance of the 29th Division. This photograph was taken on 20 July. (*NARA*)

(**Opposite, above**) Witscher photographed the task force from the 29th Division entering the Carrefour de la Bascule at the eastern end of Saint-Lô (Benamou, *Normandy 1944*, p. 121). Although the image is dated 19 July, the banner of the 1/115th Infantry on the café-restaurant has not been raised and the actual date may be 18 July (Balkoski, *Beyond the Beachhead*, pp. 269–71). (*NARA*)

(**Opposite, below**) Two tank destroyers were positioned at the Carrefour with an American casualty indicating some fighting during the advance in this photograph dated 19 July by Ryan. The banner for the first headquarters of the 1/115th Infantry has now been raised on the café-restaurant wall and was visible in this image and the following one. (*NARA*)

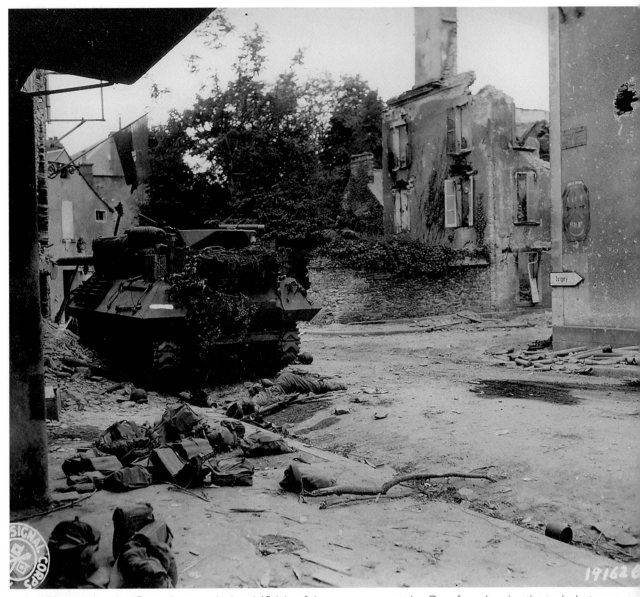

(**Above**) Another Ryan photograph dated 19 July of the same scene at the Carrefour showing the tank destroyer and an American casualty. (*NARA*)

(**Opposite, above**) A 35th Division soldier peers at the ruins of the post office in the La Dollée district of the town on 19 July (Benamou, *Normandy 1944*, p. 124) in a photograph by Musae. (*NARA*)

(**Opposite, below**) A Sherman named 'Hun Chaser' amid ruins in Saint-Lô on 20 July. The soldier in the middle distance was Private Walter Hatfield from Idaho. One of the spires of the Notre-Dame church still stood, only to be destroyed later by artillery fire (Benamou, *Normandy 1944*, p. 123). (*NARA*)

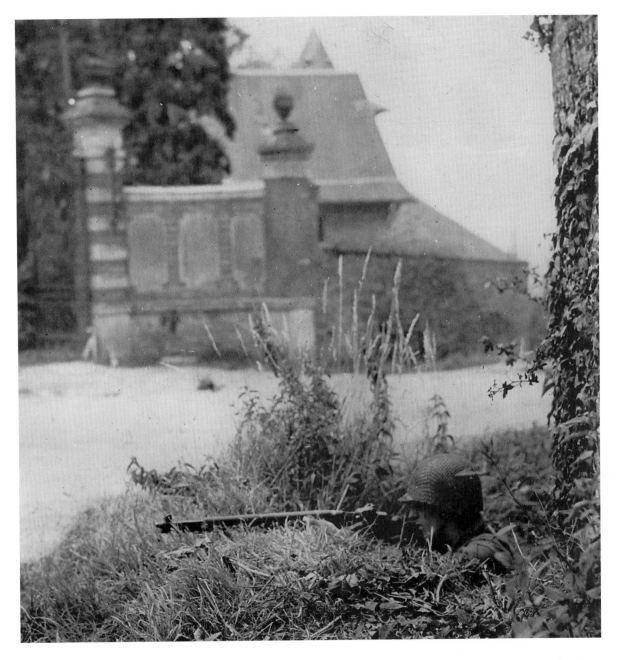

(**Opposite, above**) Infantry found it necessary to crawl at times to reduce exposure to artillery fire. Lee photographed two soldiers keeping a low profile in Saint-Lô on 20 July. (*NARA*)

(**Above**) Enemy forces remained in Saint-Lô on 20 July so actions against snipers were necessary as illustrated in a photograph by Colewell. (*NARA*)

(**Opposite, below**) German artillery fire falling in and near the town had set a truck ablaze on the same day, 20 July. The scene was photographed by Schultz. (*NARA*)

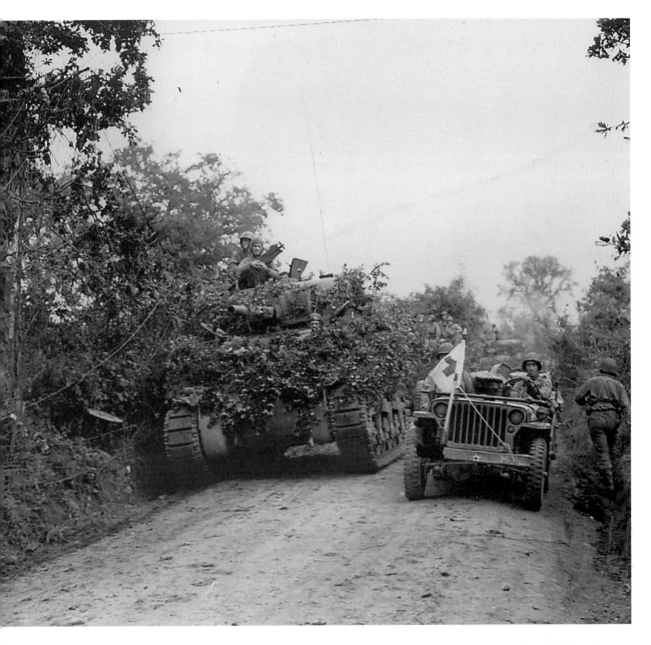

(**Opposite, above**) The Americans may have entered the town on the 19th but fighting continued. This tank destroyer fired on an enemy position on 20 July as photographed by Witscher. (*NARA*)

(**Opposite, below**) Another way of sheltering from artillery fire that continued to fall was to seek out a wall, while some remained in the alley on 23 July. (*NARA*)

(**Above**) Tanks covered with brush camouflage are passed on a road by a jeep with 5th Division medics. Collier photographed the scene on 23 July. (*NARA*)

(**Above**) Another camouflaged Sherman moving in support of infantry on 24 July as recorded by Franklin. These troops were likely assembling for the anticipated breakout during Operation Cobra. (*NARA*)

(**Opposite, above**) Enemy concrete strongpoints may have been abandoned but booby trapped or may still have harboured snipers. Dangerous work continued in the town, as photographed by Musae on 27 July. (*NARA*)

(**Opposite, below**) A view of the ruined town probably from the belfry of Notre-Dame church (Benamou, *Normandy 1944*, p. 125). (*NARA*)

191809-S

(**Above**) Artillery fire continued to fall on the town so patrols such as this one on 26 July searched the ruins for enemy artillery spotters. (*NARA*)

(**Opposite, above**) A light tank and jeep pass during the Cobra advance. (*NARA*)

(**Opposite, below**) American armour drives towards Marigny during the Cobra advance. One tank has been damaged and overturned possibly by a mine. (*NARA*)

(**Opposite, above**) Infantry from the 9th Division move through a gap in a hedgerow on 25 July at the beginning of the Cobra offensive. The hedgerow was breeched by a tank with iron bars that had been fixed to the front for the purpose. *(NARA)*

(**Opposite, below**) Soldiers from the 39th Infantry of the 9th Division enter the ruins of Hébécrevon during the Cobra advance as photographed by Kaye on 27 July. *(NARA)*

(**Above**) An exhausted soldier sleeps on a damaged street in Marigny on 28 July during Cobra. *(NARA)*

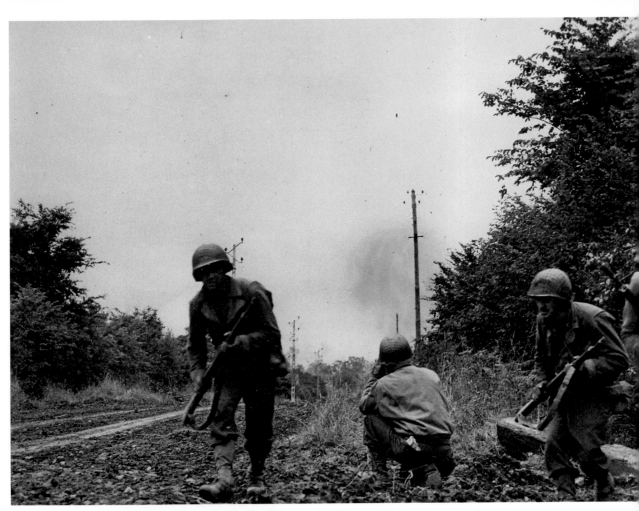

Infantry stop and observe along a road near Saint-Lô on 29 July. (*NARA*)

# Chapter Nine

# The Wounded

As with other elements of the Normandy invasion, the plan for the treatment and evacuation of the wounded – at least on Omaha Beach – was a failure. There were numerous reasons for this, principally the strength and duration of enemy resistance that was encountered. As was also the case in terms of the combat elements, particularly the infantry, improvisation became routine throughout the day.

Planned arrangements for medical treatment and evacuation were complex. Infantry companies had medics, battalions had aid stations and regiments had surgeons and medical units. In addition, a 'collecting' company from the divisional medical battalion was attached to assist each infantry regiment. In the case of the 16th, the attached company was A, 1st Medical Battalion. As discussed in an earlier chapter, this company was transported on LCI 85 and many members became casualties when the vessel was struck by artillery while attempting to land.

Naval medical units were also present and other army medical battalions had been assigned to the engineer special brigades on Omaha and Utah beaches A medical battalion possessed a 'clearing' company that would receive casualties from collecting companies and later from field and evacuation hospitals closer to the front lines. However, on D-Day the front was the beach and fields immediately beyond and no hospitals could be established.

Major Charles Tegtmeyer, 16th Infantry regimental surgeon, landed early on Easy Red close to the position of the regimental commander Colonel George Taylor:

> The wounded were hastily dressed and pulled to the shelter of the shale shelf and left with instructions to call to the landing craft for help as they grounded. I examined scores as I went, telling the men who to dress and who not to bother with. The number of dead, killed by mines, shell fragments, machine guns and sniper bullets was appalling … We followed the Colonel and covered a thousand yards of [beach], just asking for it. Father Deery was having a busy day too, for many of the men had more need of him than of me.

Eventually the 16th Medical Detachment established its aid station at the E-2 exit near the regimental command post in the limited shelter just below the bluff crest. His men spent the afternoon going down to the beach below them; in one instance Sergeants

Ed Bailey and Bernie Friedenberg followed an engineer with a mine detector into the grass at the base of the slope to retrieve a man who had stepped on a mine. Eight mines were removed before they reached the man who had two broken legs.

The arrival of 26th Infantry in the evening was a particularly welcome event. The 3/26th commander Lieutenant Colonel John Corley stopped by the aid station and expressed concern for the wounded that numbered eighty-four at that time. Within a short period about 100 of Corley's soldiers had surrendered their blankets to cover the wounded. After darkness Tegtmeyer moved many of his wounded down to the ruined house near the beach but the promised evacuation craft never arrived. Of those more seriously wounded who remained at the aid station, five died during the night and four more were lost that morning before evacuation began.[73]

Other medical detachments had trying experiences both approaching the beach and following landing. The 643rd Medical Clearing Company (61st Medical Battalion) was an element of the 5th Engineer Special Brigade and was not able to land on Easy Red until afternoon. They immediately began to rescue wounded in danger of drowning in the surf on a beach described as under constant artillery, mortar and sniper fire. Ultimately casualties from the beach were moved to a clearing station established in a German casemate on the hillside near E-3, evidently WN 62. Gathering of casualties from areas including minefields continued after darkness fell.

Another portion of the 643rd eventually landed under fire on Dog White sector in the early afternoon. Their efforts were devoted to gathering wounded for evacuation by landing craft or Dukws. One such Dukw was struck by artillery fire after wounded had been placed aboard: 'the driver and casualties were blown to pieces and the loaders were hit by flying debris.' By 1700 a clearing station had been established in the anti-tank ditch near E-1 and treatment proceeded using salvaged supplies.[74]

The headquarters detachment of the 61st Medical Battalion landed on Easy Red and attempted to move east to Fox Green but were stopped by debris and the cries of wounded soldiers. Since they were mainly clerks they had landed with typewriters and forms and had no medical supplies. They were forced to scrounge first-aid packets from wounded or dead soldiers. In numerous instances they found those packets had been replaced with candy and cigarettes. They contended that some soldiers called for assistance with injuries that could have been dealt with by the soldiers themselves. They had moved only a short distance when they sought shelter in a small defile. They continued to scrounge supplies including blood plasma from an LST and commandeered a jeep to carry wounded to the shelter of the defile. By 2200 (roughly dusk) the fire had quieted and a station was established on the hill. The beach in their vicinity was cleared of wounded by midnight but earlier some wounded were evacuated in a small boat, the only evacuation to occur in this area.[75]

The situation on Utah Beach proceeded more smoothly due to the comparative lack of enemy opposition. The first evacuations were conducted by Naval Beach

Medical sections before arrival of two companies from the 261st Medical Battalion (1st Engineer Special Brigade) with attached surgical teams. Later in the day the three collecting companies of the 4th Medical Battalion of the 4th Infantry Division disembarked with most of their ambulances.[76]

The treatment of the airborne casualties inland was a matter of concern, reflected in comments by Marshall (see Chapter Two) about the contrast between expectations of wounded paratroopers compared with other infantry. Medical units at Utah Beach were informed on the afternoon of 7 June that the 307th Airborne Medical Company (82nd Airborne) had approximately 300 casualties in its care and scant supplies with which to treat them. These included jump or glider-landing injuries and battle wounds. Three days would pass before effective medical assistance arrived at the more inland locations of the 82nd Airborne, resulting in numerous deaths in the opinion of Lieutenant Colonel Edward Krause of the 3/505th.[77]

General Bradley visited a casualty station near Utah on 7 June, probably one of the collecting companies of the 261st Medical Battalion. On that day Company C of the battalion treated seventy-one casualties and evacuated 696, while twenty-one of the soldiers died.[78]

> About forty cases lying on litters outside, covered with blankets await evacuation. Inside the tents there were about sixty non-transportable cases. Many of them serious. Some initial shortage of whole blood but that was repaired and things were functioning smoothly. GIs washing out sheets for sterile operations, large buckets of blood stained bandages, a German young soldier sitting on a litter by himself ignored by the GIs …

Bradley asked the doctor if he had everything he needed and if evacuation was proceeding smoothly. When the soldiers realized the commander of First Army was present, they were eager to speak with him. One man 'lifted his bloodstained head from the cot' and mentioned he was in the 82nd Airborne, which Bradley had once commanded.

> General smiled, put his hand on the youngster's [shoulder], '325th regiment.' 'Yessir,' the soldier answered, 'that's still my regiment.' He was hurt in a glider crash. Another soldier showed general where an S-mine hit him in the foot. Third plucky corporal with the bloody stump of a leg, talked to the general, said 'He guessed he felt better, Sir. – We've got to take our casualties in the airborne – that's part of war.' … Another row of prisoners but the general ignored them.[79]

In terms of numbers, admissions to First US Army hospitals in the first two months totaled 95,172. These admissions included 32,699 lightly wounded (thirty-one of whom died) and 27,580 seriously wounded (2,027 of whom died). The remainder consisted of injuries, illnesses and neuropsychiatric cases.

The upper and lower extremities were most commonly injured (57–61 per cent) followed by chest (10–11 per cent), neurological (about 7 per cent), face and jaw (5–6 per cent) and abdomen/buttocks (8–10 per cent). Slightly more than one-third of the soldiers had been wounded in two or more places.

Wounds to the chest, head or spine and abdomen or buttocks posed threats to major organs or raised the possibility of paralysis or peritonitis. Major Haynes, the First Army neurosurgeon, arrived on the beach on D+4. He operated on twenty-one soldiers, nineteen of whom survived to be evacuated. Soldiers with mandibles shot away faced particular difficulties from respiratory distress. One such patient died while being transported to the air strip for evacuation. All subsequent patients received a tracheotomy and survived evacuation either by ship or airplane.[80] Such incidents reveal the frequent adjustments and developments to army medical procedures that occurred.

Gun shots and artillery shells were the most common causes of wounds, with the former reduced from 33 per cent to 24 per cent June to July while artillery or mortar wounds increased from 51 per cent to 60 per cent during the two months. Bomb wounds were low (4–6 per cent) due to the infrequent raids by the Luftwaffe. Burn injuries arriving in hospitals were even fewer (around 1 per cent) but did increase slightly in July as armoured combat became more common. However, many tank crewmen who were burned may not have survived to reach an aid station or hospital.

Neuropsychiatric or NP admissions – also called combat exhaustion – to First Army hospitals numbered 11,150 cases; 9,101 of these occurred in July. The proportions relative to all admissions increased from 6 per cent to nearly 15 per cent in July. The relative proportions were lower in airborne divisions, with ratios of wounded to combat exhaustion cases between 10:1 and 12:1 in the 82nd Airborne and 19:1 in the 101st. The veteran 9th Division had nearly one NP case for every fourteen wounded in June but their hard fighting during the advance to Cherbourg and then southwards into Normandy increased combat exhaustion cases to one in seven.

The 29th Infantry had 287 NP cases (7:1) in June but those increased dramatically to 1,027 in July (3:1). Similar changes were indicated in the 30th Division (June about 9:1 to 3.5:1 in July). The hard fighting in the interior particularly during the advance to Saint-Lô had exacted its toll on the divisions. The First US Army Report acknowledged the increase in neuropsychiatric cases reflected a landscape filled with hedgerows and other terrain difficulties, wet and muddy conditions and stiff enemy resistance near Carentan, La Haye-du-Puits and Saint-Lô.

Admissions for combat exhaustion were consistent with pre-invasion plans during the first week in Normandy but quickly exceeded those expectations. Army medical staffs created 'exhaustion centers' that allowed soldiers to relax and sleep, often with the chemical assistance of sodium amytol sometimes referred to as 'blue 88s'. Army doctors believed it was essential that soldiers be returned to their units as quickly as possible, but this view was not always appreciated and led to antagonistic attitudes towards the returning soldiers. Several divisions, including the 29th and 30th, established exhaustion centers at the divisional level. By the end of July 6,940 had been returned to duty while 3,121 had to be evacuated to the United Kingdom.

Minor wounds that were thought to be self-inflicted posed another concern although one of much smaller scale. Medical staff identified 848 cases of which 625 were cleared of any accusations. Twenty-four individuals were returned to their units for disciplinary action and 199 soldiers remained under suspicion in late July.[81]

Ellis has written eloquently on the levels of casualties during the Second World War and particularly on the disproportionate burden that fell upon the infantry. A US Army survey of certain rifle companies in four infantry divisions (1st, 4th, 9th and 29th) that bore the burden from the outset in Normandy revealed nearly 60 per cent of enlisted soldiers and 69 per cent of their officers became casualties during the first two months. One officer in the 30th Division estimated 90 per cent of the rifle platoon soldiers in that division were killed, wounded or missing during the battle for Saint-Lô.[82]

There were various reasons why the survival of wounded soldiers increased in certain theatres during the Second World War, with the introduction of new medicines being principal among them. Several had been developed just before the war or had been placed in wide usage during the conflict. Treatments with sulfa drugs and penicillin to prevent the spread of infection and plasma or preferably whole blood to address the major threat of shock were material to increased survival rates.[83]

Blood plasma (dehydrated white blood cells) was rehydrated with sterile water in the field and did not require refrigeration. The value of plasma in saving lives was demonstrated in the case of a soldier with a chest wound on a D-Day beach. The first two bottles lacked sufficient vacuum to draw sterile water into the plasma. The third was more successful and in a few minutes the soldier's pulse revived and he felt better. The First Army medical report noted that plasma while plentiful was not a substitute for whole blood. One of the 3rd Auxiliary Surgical team leaders stated,

> In this campaign we believe the greatest single blessing from the medical point of view has been the availability of blood bank blood. In contrast to the African and Sicilian campaigns, we are now able to operate upon and save patients that could never have survived on plasma alone.

Penicillin was considered particularly effective in preventing the spread of wound infection but did not prevent the onset of gas gangrene. For about two weeks in June, supplies of penicillin were so low that its use in clearing stations was disrupted. The problem was solved with air shipments from the United States.[84]

Chances for survival increased dramatically if a soldier received treatment quickly at an aid station or field hospital. As soon as field hospitals were established major surgical procedures ceased at the clearing stations. The practice of placing field hospitals close to the battle front was heartily endorsed since it was considered to have saved many lives. Those field hospitals closer to the front had a higher mortality rate since some seriously wounded patients admitted would have died during transport to rear areas.

Wounds to the abdomen or chest/abdomen and major chest trauma were often considered non-transportable and required treatment as soon as possible. The 643rd Medical Clearing Company argued much confusion arose from policies of not transporting perforating chest and abdominal wounds for seven days and not evacuating abdominal wound cases by air. As the campaign progressed all such wounds were evacuated by air from the Omaha area with success.[85]

Greater influxes of casualties and consequent higher admission rates such as during the advance on Saint-Lô strained hospital capacity and resulted in higher mortality rates. Patients often had to wait longer for surgical procedures. Since those recovering from shock could not always receive surgical treatment at optimal moments, some would slip back into shock and not recover. If wounds were not debrided or fully cleaned quickly, bacteria might result in gas gangrene.[86]

Transport to England by air was another means of securing advanced care more quickly. The air strip on the bluff behind Easy Red was opened on 10 June and evacuations began immediately. Many of the patients from the Omaha sector were transported back to England in this manner. Sea transport remained the primary means of evacuation from Utah and the Cotentin until late July, although patients were carried in ambulances to the Easy Red air strip in late June when the Channel storm disrupted sea traffic.

(**Opposite, above**) A medical officer from the 82nd Airborne Division offers a cigarette to a wounded German prisoner, perhaps as an inducement to provide information. The soldier on the left appears to be an intelligence officer interrogating the prisoner since he is writing in a small book. Witscher recorded the photograph on 7 June as the division was fighting to consolidate its position around Sainte-Mère-Église. (*NARA*)

(**Opposite, below**) Witscher photographed jeep evacuation of 82nd Airborne wounded from Sainte-Mère-Église on 12 June. German prisoners are visible near the building in the background. (*NARA*)

(**Opposite, above**) 'A field hospital somewhere in Northern France operates efficiently as Medics bring in casualties from the beachheads. The hospital treats both American and British troops. France, June 9, 1944, 8th Inf. Regt., 4th Inf. Div.' The caption does not mention that at least one of the wounded photographed by Shelton was German (lower right with rank chevron on sleeve). The location was probably inland from Utah Beach but might be the clearing station for the 4th Medical Battalion that opened on 8–9 June just south of Beuzeville close to Sainte-Mère-Église (*First US Army Report Operations 20 Oct 43–1 Aug 44*, VII, p. 67). (*NARA*)

(**Opposite, below**) Omar Bradley greets George Marshall (Army Chief of Staff) and Henry (Hap) Arnold (Army Air Corps commander) at Exit E-1 on 12 June. Chet Hansen, an aide to Bradley, described the moment in his diary: 'We loaded them on Recce cars, headed up to the airstrip where they dismounted, entered an aircraft and talked to the nurse adjusting the patients for movement to England. Hap Arnold seemed well pleased with airfield. Marshall generally seemed quite happy with progress of events though he spoke little and seldom smiled...' (*NARA*)

(**Above, left**) Aerial view of the air strip behind Easy Red that opened on 10 June. The photograph was an early one recorded before the runway expansion as seen in Chapter 6. Fighter planes were present on the runway. The original caption noted roughly 1,000 foxholes excavated into the Norman chalk around the air strip. (*NARA*)

(**Above, right**) A modern view of the fields with the approximate location of the air strip outlined. The image indicates a white patch as the only surface trace of the runway although the field contours also provide some evidence. (*Google Earth*)

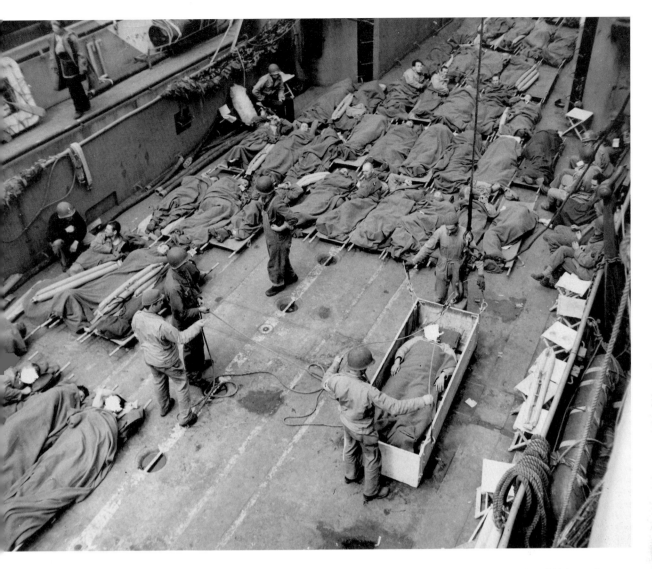

(**Opposite, above**) The air strip on the bluff behind Easy Red had only been open a few days when Weintraub photographed the evacuation of wounded by C-47. Bradley commented that thousands of wounded were transported to hospitals in England in this manner. A holding station established by the 643rd Medical Collecting Company was finally closed at the end of August, by which time 23,615 patients had been evacuated by air (annual report, p. 8). (*NARA*)

(**Opposite, below**) Casualties were fortunate if they were quickly transported to offshore vessels or planes. These wounded, including members of the 101st Airborne Division, are being evacuated by sea. Dressings reflect injuries to extremities and crania. (*NARA*)

(**Above**) Soldiers being transferred to an LCT in a photograph dated 11 June. The wounded included at least one member of the 101st Airborne Division. The use of coffin-like wooden boxes for transport cannot have been good for morale. Censors have obscured some of the faces. (*NARA*)

Four neurosurgeons –
Captains Gillespie, Plant,
Donne and Second Lieutenant
Clow – operate in Normandy.
Major Haynes, First Army
neurosurgeon, operated on
twenty-one patients, nineteen
of whom survived (643rd
Medical Company annual
report p. 7). (NARA)

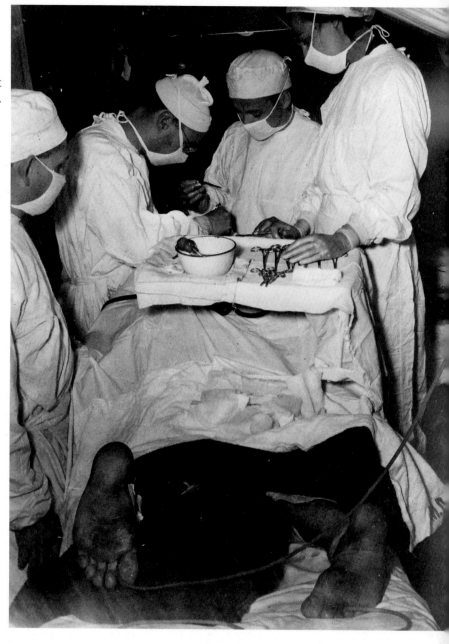

(**Opposite, above**) Surgical procedure at the 128th Evacuation Hospital opened 11 June near Boutteville inland from Utah Beach. The arm board created to provide support for sodium pentathol syringes was discussed in the annual report of the 643rd Medical Clearing Company (p. 13). (NARA)

(**Opposite, below**) Weintraub photographed a group of nurses wearing First Army patches gathering for a meal on 15 June in Normandy. The arrival of nurses was much appreciated by army medical staffs as a means of providing order and discipline in hospital routine and particularly for the continuing care offered to patients. (NARA)

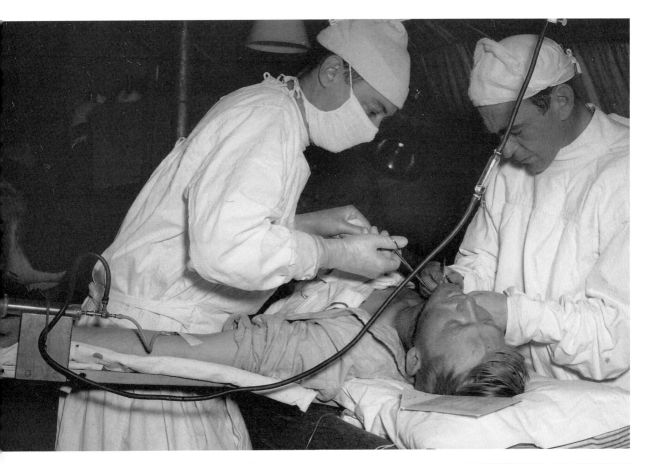

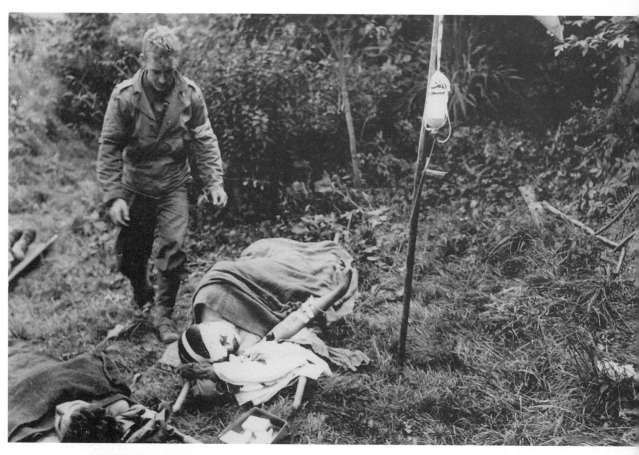

(**Opposite, above**) A photograph by Cunningham of plasma being administered at an aid post. The dehydrated white blood cells did not need to be refrigerated. Field use of plasma rehydrated with sterile water helped prevent shock and saved many lives. (*NARA*)

(**Opposite, below**) Wounded soldiers in a jeep await treatment probably at a field hospital. Chaplin Sydney Broom from Rhode Island was standing near the wounded. The image was recorded north of Saint-Lô probably in late June. (*NARA*)

(**Above**) Several medics from the 79th Division administer plasma to a wounded soldier on 7 July. (*NARA*)

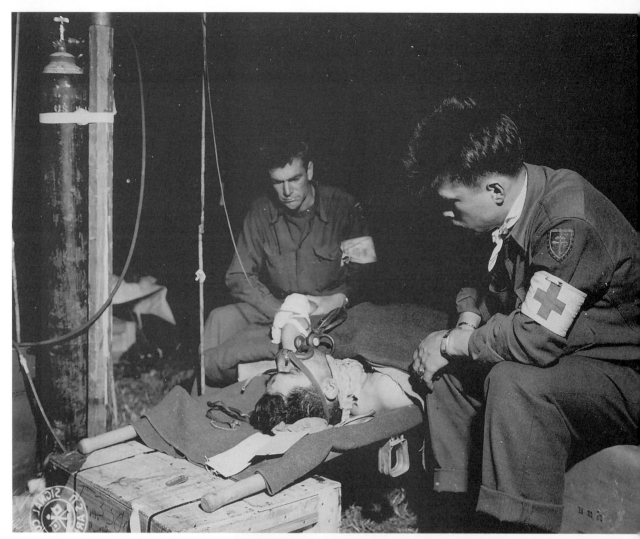

Medics at a 79th Division hospital administer oxygen to Private First Class Platte from Louisiana on 8 July in a photograph by Gallo. (*NARA*)

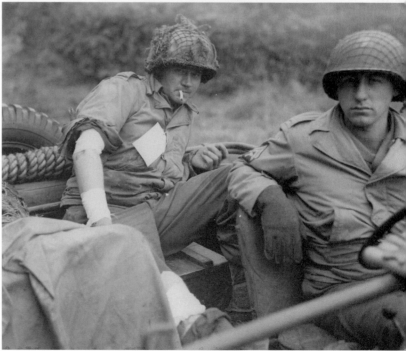

Private Vincent Lucas from Braddock, Pennsylvania, waits outside a collecting station on 11 July as photographed by Carolan. (*NARA*)

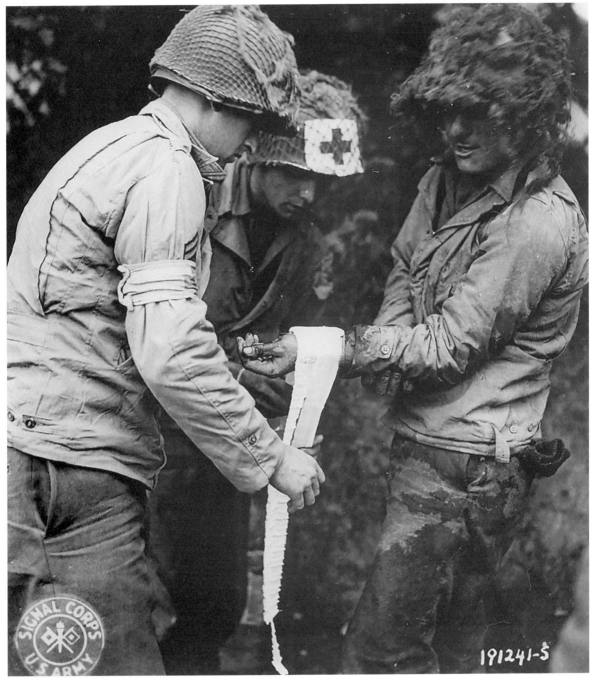

Private Paul Leone from New Britain, Connecticut, receives treatment for an injured hand on 11 July. (*NARA*)

Soldiers removed Captain John Strader of the 35th Division from the hedgerows by stretcher after he was wounded on 21 July, as recorded by Lapine. (*NARA*)

Witscher photographed an injured German soldier being lifted into a half-track on 20 July. (NARA)

Runyan photographed a group of German prisoners including a medic transporting one of their own wounded near La Chappelle in late July. (NARA)

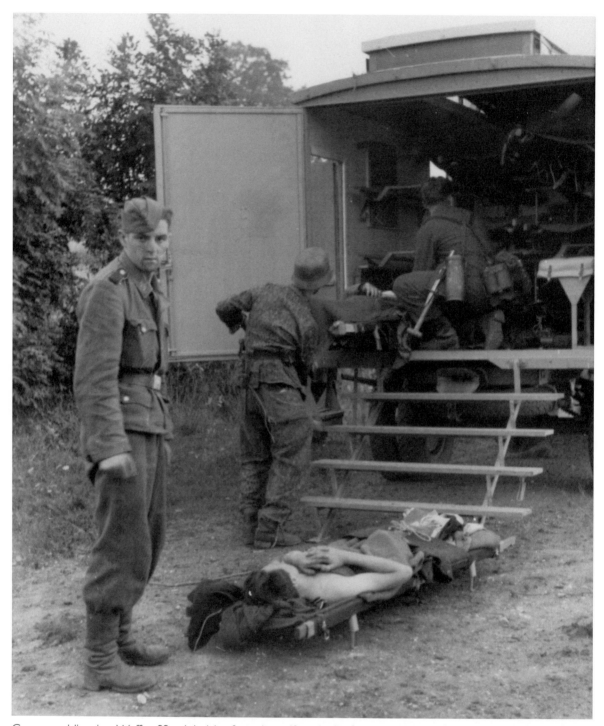

German soldiers in a Waffen-SS unit judging from the uniform in the foreground and perhaps the camouflage outfit in the rear. A Luftwaffe soldier was present in the medical transport truck. Theobald photographed them loading wounded comrades on the vehicle during the summer of 1944. *(Bundesarchiv)*

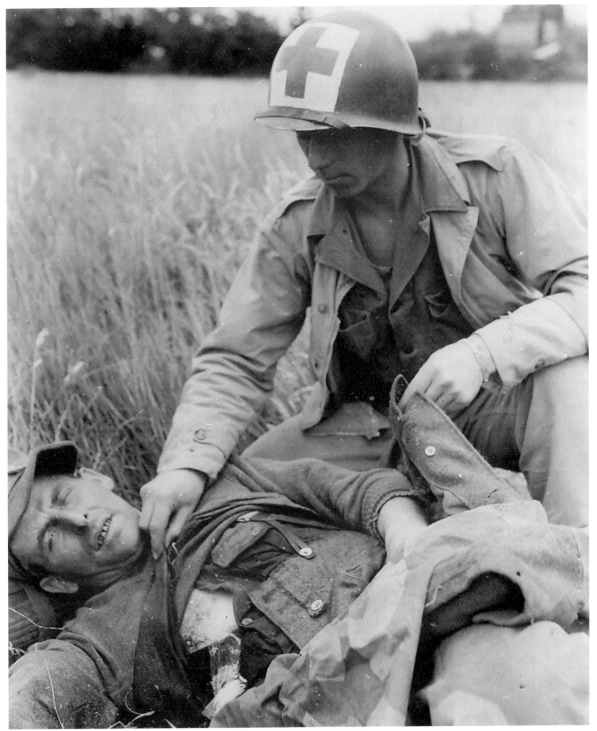

A medic examines a wounded or dead German soldier near Coutances. Wilkes photographed the scene on 31 July during the Cobra advance. (*NARA*)

# Chapter Ten

# The Dead and Their Cemeteries

Provisions for soldiers who were killed in combat or who died from their wounds at aid stations or evacuation hospitals were commenced almost immediately. Soldiers and sailors succumbed in many ways on D-Day and during the campaign. Some men initially listed as missing on the beaches were found to have drowned, while others later returned to their units or were discovered to have become prisoners of war for a brief period.

During the campaign, men were lost in strange or accidental circumstances. The 643rd Medical Clearing Company admitted twenty-one patients with acute alcohol poisoning from drinking a mixture of fruit juice and cleaning fluid or denatured alcohol, eleven of whom died shortly after admission.[87] On 25 June the 505th Parachute Infantry reported that planes believed to be American P-47 fighter-bombers strafed and dropped bombs on regimental positions, killing Sergeant W. Bensch and Private Herb Dempsey and injuring Sergeant Ralph Warwick all from Company C. Two days later the 508th Parachute Infantry reported it downed a Cub observation plane with an 81mm mortar shell, killing both occupants. On 28 June the 506th Parachute Infantry had been moved to a rear area but that evening the truck carrying the regimental collection of captured German arms and ammunition exploded. Two soldiers and one civilian were killed and five other soldiers were injured.

Most died directly or indirectly as a result of military action with the enemy. Lieutenant Colonel Herbert Hicks commanded the 2nd Battalion of the 16th Infantry. On the afternoon of 7 June he asked the regimental headquarters for some Graves Registration units, stating, 'There are dead all along the road between you and me and this isn't good for the morale.'[88] These men were probably among the first interments in the new cemetery on the bluff between exits E-1 and E-3. That same day burials began further to the west at a temporary cemetery on the Dog White sector of Omaha Beach.

Injured and dead paratroopers and transport craft crew were of course scattered across the Cotentin following the D-Day drop and their recovery would take some time. A major in the 506th Parachute Infantry discovered the remains of a crashed transport plane on 9 June with 'four bodies burned beyond recognition – 17 hooks on static line indicated stick had jumped.' Two days later the 3/505th reminded the regimental command that the bodies of three paratroopers had been reported three days ago and requested a guide presumably for recovery.[89]

The 82nd Airborne established a divisional cemetery 300 yards west of the Les Forges road junction near Blosville on D+1, the same junction shown in the photograph of gliders landing early on that day, 7 June. Therefore, the men who were killed in glider landings on the evening of D-Day or the following morning were close to their first place of interment.

During the summer campaign in 1944 the Americans created numerous cemeteries around the battlefields of Normandy, including one for the 29th Division near the village of La Cambe on 10 June. The burying ground remained open until the spring of 1945 but was never considered suitable for permanent occupation due to its poor location and landscape alterations such as hedge removals. As a consequence, more than 4,000 American fallen were repatriated or moved to Saint-Laurent. The German dead at Saint-Laurent were moved to La Cambe. The *Volksbund Deutsche Kriegsgräberfürsorge* or German War Graves Commission ultimately assumed control of La Cambe, which became their largest cemetery in Normandy with more than 21,000 burials.[90]

Ultimately these early burial grounds were closed in favour of two permanent ones behind Omaha Beach and near the town of Saint-James in Brittany that are now maintained by the American Battle Monuments Commission. The British Commonwealth War Graves Commission chose to maintain their earliest burial areas, resulting in many more cemeteries of varying and often smaller size. Some of the Commonwealth grounds still contain burials of German soldiers.

The cemetery of Orglandes on the Cotentin was created on 19 June by the US First Army exclusively for German dead. Several of the American cemeteries also held burials of German soldiers. Some such as Sainte-Mère-Église had a dedicated section for enemy burials. These burials were often left behind when the Americans vacated the locations. In the case of Sainte-Mère-Église, both cemeteries had been intended as permanent locations but the nearly 8,000 enemy dead outnumbered the nearly 7,000 American burials and a decision was made to abandon the location in February 1946. The US burials were moved to Saint-Laurent or were repatriated while the German remains were moved to one of their burial grounds.

The Americans established a cemetery near Marigny on 1 August where the troops killed in the mistaken bombing by Allied planes at the beginning of Operation Cobra were buried. The location was soon opened for those killed in the battles around Saint-Lô. Eventually all of the more than 3,000 burials were repatriated or moved. However, Germans had also been buried in a separate cemetery at Marigny and their War Graves Commission assumed control of the location.[91]

The cemeteries will remain the most enduring landscapes of the Normandy Campaign. Differences in design between American, British/Canadian and German styles of commemoration are marked and complex, as reflected in the grave markers. Headstones in both the American Battle Monuments Commission and Commonwealth War Graves Commission cemeteries mark individual graves. There are similarities between them: the date of death, military rank and the military unit of the deceased are noted. In the Commonwealth cemeteries, headstones bear the elaborate regimental crests while American ones provide the state of origin. In addition, Stars of David are used where appropriate. The Allied headstones mark individual graves but references to state and battalion or regiment establish a unity of association and purpose.

Gravestones in the cemeteries maintained by the *Volksbund Deutsche Kriegsgräberfürsorge* mark the graves of several persons that are identified by name, military rank, dates of birth and death when known, although many are unidentified. No mention of military unit is provided. In addition, different stone types and orientations provide a sense of diversity. The German graves are collective but emphasize the life span of the individual with no reference to membership in a particular army division. This emphasis upon the individual may consciously or unconsciously reinforce the view that ultimate responsibility for monstrous military and political acts lay with the Nazi Party and certain fanatical army units. Such apportionment of responsibility would hold that German soldiers were as much victims of Fascism as were the Allied soldiers and European citizens who died. These attitudes reflect major philosophical perspectives in postwar Germany and are reflected in a bilingual brochure available at the German cemeteries in Normandy.[92] Perhaps this point is overemphasized since burial stones placed in Germany during the war also did not mention military unit, although the letters SS and the swastika were used on temporary markers in Normandy.

(**Opposite, above**) A D-Day casualty lying next to a log obstacle, photographed on Dog White sector probably on 7 June. His location was marked by crossed M1 and M1903 rifles. Compare the bump on the bluff at left with the 12 June photograph on page 208 of the cemetery on Dog White. (*NARA*)

(**Opposite, below**) Paratroopers await identification and burial perhaps near Sainte-Mère-Église in a Spangle photograph on 7 June. That location would suggest they were 505th Parachute Infantry casualties. (*NARA*)

(**Above**) A crashed glider and one of its occupants were photographed by Runyan on 7 June. The remains of a jeep were visible in the wreckage. Glider transport was considered risky by airborne troops. The assistant commander of the 101st Airborne, Brigadier General Don Pratt, was killed in a glider crash on D-Day. (*NARA*)

(**Opposite, above**) American casualties in a field near the landing beaches judging from the barrage balloons on the skyline. These soldiers may be early interments in the Saint-Laurent cemetery on the eastern bluff above Exit E-1. (*NARA*)

(**Opposite, below**) Montgomery photographed airborne casualties lying in a hedgerow ditch near Sainte-Marie-du-Mont on 12 June. (*NARA*)

(**Opposite, above**) A memorial service was held at the first American cemetery on Dog White sector and was photographed by Bowen on 12 June. The bluff line is the same as shown in the earlier photograph of the soldier lying near the log obstacle. (*NARA*)

(**Opposite, below**) Todd photographed this German soldier who was killed by the African American patrol on 10 June that was illustrated earlier in the volume. (*NARA*)

(**Above**) Weintraub recorded a group of civilians with a dead German on 13 June. The Frenchman at right killed the soldier who had compelled him to work for a few francs daily. (*NARA*)

(**Above**) A French couple prays for an American casualty who has been covered with flowers. Himes photographed the scene on 17 June. (*NARA*)

(**Opposite, above**) Major Thomas Howie commanded the 3/116th and was killed outside Saint-Lô. His body was placed on the rubble of Sainte-Croix church in town. Schultz recorded this photograph on 20 July. (*NARA*)

(**Opposite, below**) American soldiers pass Germans during the advance from Saint-Lô on 26 July. (*NARA*)

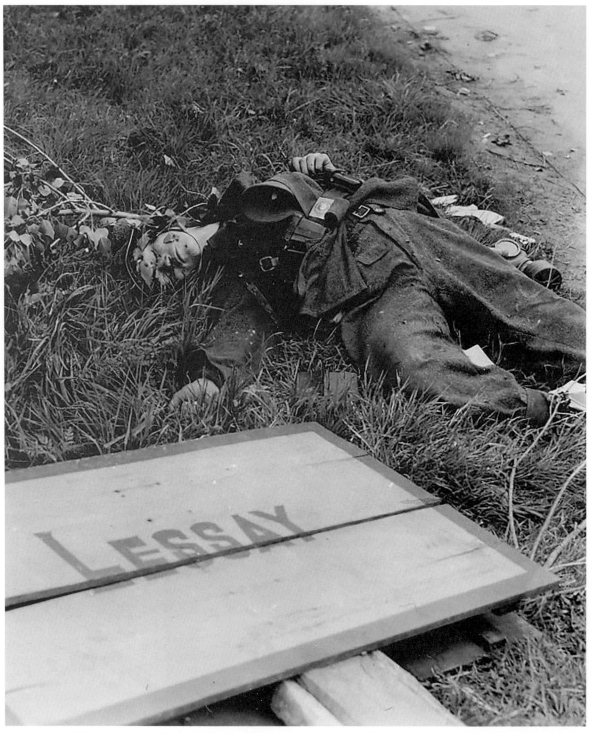

A German soldier who was killed on the road between Lessay and Coutances during the Cobra advance was photographed on 28 July. *(NARA)*

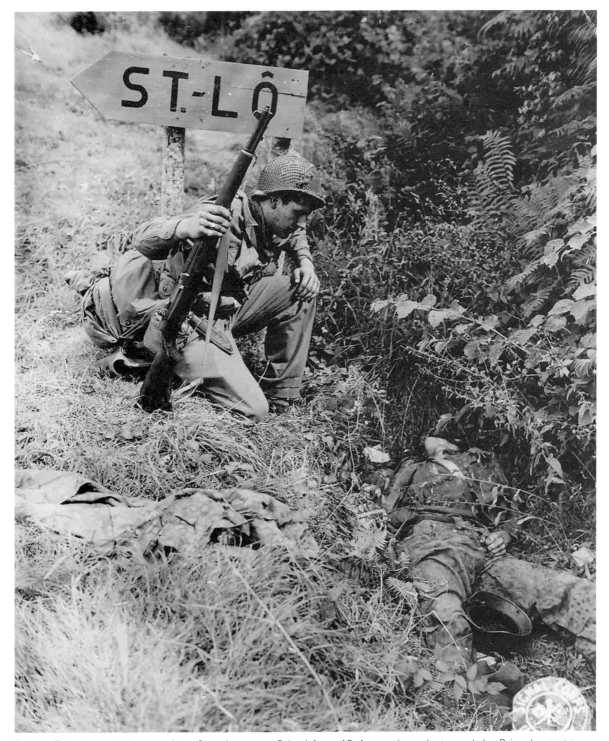

Private Futz stares at the remains of a sniper near Saint-Lô on 15 August in a photograph by Brignolo. *(NARA)*

(**Opposite, above**) A cemetery at Blosville near Sainte-Mère-Église was established for the 82nd Airborne Division on 7 June. By 16 June 530 soldiers had been interred. This image was recorded on 20 June. A nearby cemetery was opened on 27 June for soldiers from the VIII Corps on the Cotentin Peninsula (*Graves Registration*, p. 32). (*NARA*)

(**Opposite, below**) A modern view of the former location of the cemetery facing east. Some of the glider landings on 7 June occurred near the crossroads just behind the tree line (see Chapter 3).

(**Above**) A temporary cemetery for the 101st Airborne Division was opened at Hiesville shortly after D-Day (*Graves Registration*, pp. 32–3). Montgomery recorded a soldier from the 101st on 9 June guarding German prisoners digging graves possibly for their own casualties as indicated in the original caption but perhaps for Americans. Parallel lines of string have been laid out to create rows. (*NARA*)

192353

(**Opposite, above**) The same location appears in the background of a field near Sainte-Marie-du-Mont – probably Hiesville – in a photograph attributed to Runyan on 7 June. In the foreground a chaplain offered prayers for members of the 101st wrapped in parachutes who were killed early in the campaign. (*NARA*)

(**Opposite, below**) A cemetery for the 29th Division was created on 10 June near the inland village of La Cambe. This photograph shows the location on 13 June. When the burials were relocated to the permanent one at Colleville, German soldiers continued to be buried in the cemetery. (*NARA*)

(**Above**) A modern view of the German cemetery at La Cambe.

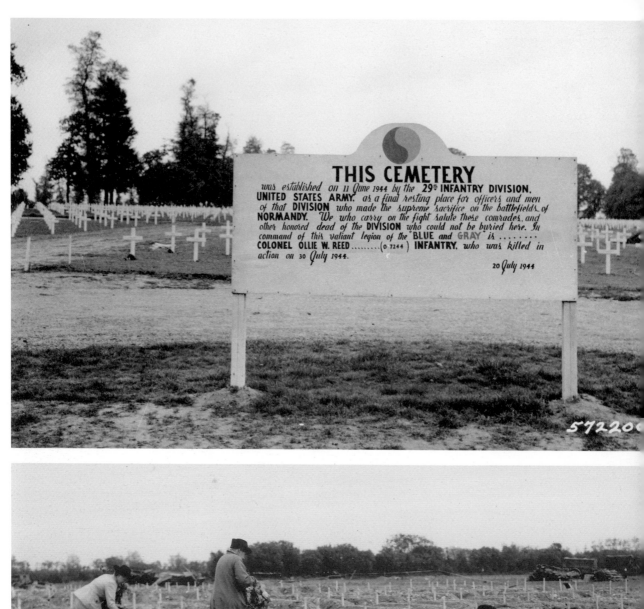

THIS CEMETERY
was established on 11 June 1944 by the 29th INFANTRY DIVISION, UNITED STATES ARMY, as a final resting place for officers and men of that DIVISION who made the supreme sacrifice on the battlefields of NORMANDY. We who carry on the fight salute these comrades, and other honored dead of the DIVISION who could not be buried here. In command of this valiant legion of the BLUE and GRAY is ........ COLONEL OLLIE W. REED ........(O-7244) INFANTRY, who was killed in action on 30 July 1944.
20 July 1944

(**Opposite, above**) American burials continued at La Cambe until April 1945, by which time 4,534 soldiers had been interred (*Graves Registration*, p. 34). This image of the temporary dedication marker was recorded in 1945. (*NARA*)

(**Opposite, below**) 'Doing the Job for American Mothers. French ladies from villages around Normandy, France, place flowers on the graves of American soldiers who gave their lives on the beachheads and in front line assaults on the continent, June 20, 1944.' Saint-Laurent cemetery was opened on 10 June; by 26 June burials of 1,510 Americans, 48 Allies and 606 enemy soldiers had occurred (*Graves Registration*, p. 31). The graves were marked by vertical sticks bearing identification tags. (*NARA*)

(**Above**) Private Ortega from Los Angeles paints crosses for use as grave markers on 7 July. (*NARA*)

(**Opposite, above**) Weintraub photographed German prisoners digging graves on 4 August probably at Saint-Laurent. They seemed happy to be out of the war. *(NARA)*

(**Opposite, below**) Another view by Weintraub recorded on the same day, 4 August. Saint-Laurent was officially closed in late July, by which time 3,797 Americans had been buried (*Graves Registration*, p. 31). New rows were being laid out; wooden crosses have replaced the vertical sticks. *(NARA)*

(**Above**) Many American cemeteries were opened in Normandy during the summer of 1944. A ceremony on Bastille Day 1944 was held at Sainte-Mère-Église cemetery No. 2 on the western edge of the town. *(NARA)*

508608

 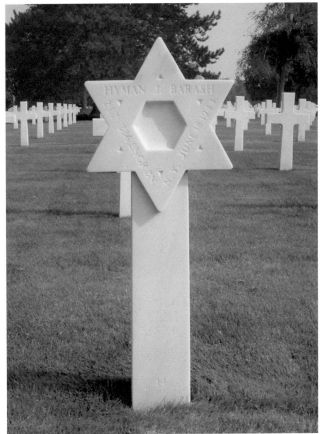

(**Opposite, above**) A view of Sainte-Mère-Église cemetery No. 2 on the second anniversary of D-Day recorded by Tobey. The various temporary burying grounds were eventually abandoned, with burials moved to Saint-Laurent that was redesigned and named the Normandy American Cemetery near Colleville. Others were reinterred at Saint-James in Brittany while more than half of the remains were repatriated to the United States. (*NARA*)

(**Opposite, below**) An aerial view of the redesigned cemetery at Colleville facing south recorded by Ray in May 1957. The first troops leaving Easy Red sector on D-Day morning moved inland through the hedgerow-bordered fields south of the cemetery. (*NARA*)

(**Above, left**) The marker at Colleville for Second Lieutenant Turner Turnbull who was killed on 7 June, the day following the gallant stand by members of Company D of the 505th Parachute Infantry at Neuville-au-Plain.

(**Above, right**) The Star of David marker at Colleville for Second Lieutenant Hyman Barash of the 336th Engineer Combat Battalion who died on 18 June.

(**Above, left**) The marker at the British War Cemetery at Ryes for Sergeant S.L. Wright, age 36, of the Green Howards who was killed on 6 June.

(**Above, right**) The marker for Sergeant Harry Greenfield, age 33, from an anti-tank battery in the 79th Armoured Division who was killed on 29 June and buried at Fontenay-le-Pesnil.

(**Opposite, above**) The British War Cemetery at Fontenay-le-Pesnil facing into the Norman countryside.

(**Opposite, below left**) A horizontal marker at La Cambe for Grenadier Otto Scherhäufer, age 19, who died on 12 August, and Oberpionier Gustav Jäkel, age 18, who died on 16 July.

(**Opposite, below right**) A vertical marker at Orglandes for Kanonier Walter Klug, age 38, killed on 6 June, Unteroffizier Heinz Otto, age 27, killed on 21 June and an unknown soldier.

GREN.
LEO SCHERHÄUFER
*5.9.25 +12.8.44
OPION.
GUSTAV JÄKEL
*20.6.26 +16.7.44

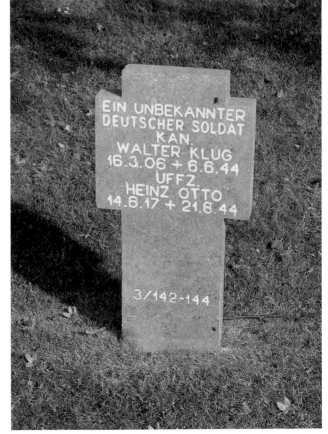

EIN UNBEKANNTER
DEUTSCHER SOLDAT
KAN.
WALTER KLUG
16.3.06 + 6.6.44
UFFZ.
HEINZ OTTO
14.6.17 + 21.6.44

3/142-144

A monument to a C-47 crew and sixteen 82nd Airborne paratroopers near Picauville on the Cotentin. The plane was lost early on the morning of 6 June.

A monument commemorating the location of the former cemetery at Blosville.

ICI
REPOSÈRENT
DE JUIN 1944
A 1948
6000 SOLDATS
AMÉRICAINS
TOMBÉS
POUR LA
LIBÉRATION
DE LA
FRANCE

9th Infantry Division
79th Infantry Division
1st Engineer Amphibious Brigade

# Chapter Eleven

# Then, Now and Then

The landscape of Omaha Beach was being modified on a daily basis and that did not change with the invasion. Some sea walls were eliminated, anti-tank ditches partially filled and beach obstacles removed starting as early as late morning on D-Day. Chet Hansen noted the changes in just a week when he returned with Bradley on 12 June to greet the American commanders.

The modern setting presents a paradox. The beach at least in its natural setting is more closely preserved at the eastern end (Fox and Easy Red). This condition is due largely to ownership by the *Conservatoire du Littoral* that has as its purpose the preservation of the natural coastal environment. The presence of the Normandy American Cemetery on the bluff above Easy Red between exits E-1 and E-3 contributed to the maintenance of the beach setting. The pathway that extends down from the cemetery overlook follows in part the route of Exit E-2 used by the 16th Infantry during their initial ascent of the bluff.

At the western end on Easy Green and Dog sectors, the continued construction of homes behind the beach has changed much of the sea front. The paradox emerges when one considers the areas above the beaches and inland. The construction of museums and the creation of the cemetery from shortly after D-Day until opening in the 1950s resulted in numerous changes to the fields behind the eastern beach sectors. Alterations have been less dramatic behind the Dog sectors, with lanes still unpaved. Hedgerow removals have continued behind Omaha as illustrated on the maps that compare the landscape then and now. These maps also include locations (filled or open triangles) for several landscape photographs.

Moving away from the more famous and heavily trafficked areas, it is possible to encounter landscapes that have changed little since 1944. This is particularly true on the Cotentin Peninsula, where fields, hedgerows and villages are largely intact and preserved battlefields from the early days of the airborne landings are present. Of course exceptions exist here also, such as on the outskirts of the enlarging town of Carentan.

The D-Day and Normandy landscapes are memorialized and symbolic places. The Normandy American Cemetery is a place of iconic significance, one featured in films such as *A Foreign Field* and *Saving Private Ryan*. It is one of several such iconic locations in Normandy.

The Normandy cemetery is the focal point of major commemorations every decade, as is the British cemetery in Bayeux maintained by the Commonwealth War Graves Commission. A hotel owner in Arromanches said in 2014 that German visitors come to Normandy, but not around 6 June. The ceremonies provide opportunities to renew ties with allies and to establish or maintain them with former foes. The importance of Omaha Beach and by extension of D-Day and the Normandy Campaign therefore lives in the present.

As a former presidential speechwriter noted, 'The beach at Normandy for Americans is a sacred spot, and when a president goes there it is a chance to lay out first principles.'[93] On 6 June 1994 Joseph Dawson who led his company into Colleville on D-Day addressed the audience at the Normandy American Cemetery with the observation, 'the battlefield had been transformed into a sanctuary that will stand forever for those who gave their lives for our country.'[94] Dawson then introduced President Bill Clinton who noted the step of the veterans may have slowed, but it must be remembered when those men were young they saved the world.

John Keegan closed his classic *Six Armies in Normandy* by leaving open the question of whether Normandy would be the last invasion of Europe. It has been said that one of the reasons for the outbreak of war across the continent in 1914 was the fact that no one was alive to remember the losses from the Napoleonic wars that ended a century earlier. If such was the case, we are entering a similar period at present. Certainly cities in Syria and Yemen have come to resemble those in Normandy in the summer of 1944 and if anything civilians are more at risk now. It is thus all the more important to remember the sacrifices in Normandy and that today they may be far greater.

Soldiers of all types were present in Normandy, from some engaged in criminal activities, to the few who seemed to genuinely enjoy combat,[95] to those who inspired others by example or spared them through acts of sacrifice. The vast majority simply sought to get through the experience alive while doing their duty without disgrace in the eyes of close comrades.

The postwar reactions of veterans have been varied. Some never visited Normandy, others waited a long time before their return, still others made frequent pilgrimages. One veteran returned every year: he walked the beach, scooped up a bit of sand and then felt he could 'go on' for another year. Among those who did not visit, memories may have profound effects. John Cotter attributed his reputation for not getting too worried about the tribulations of life 'to Normandy'. He was grateful for all the days granted afterwards.

The veterans do appreciate being remembered. Members of 299th Engineers or the 116th Infantry still lie in Normandy, in company with the paratroopers, soldiers from the 1st Division and every other unit that served in Normandy. Their family members and friends still come. In 2014 a veteran named Jack from the British

79th Armoured Division anti-tank artillery returned with his wife to visit the grave of Sergeant Harry Greenfield at Fontenay-le-Pesnel. The sergeant who served in North Africa was killed in late June in Normandy while standing near Jack.

The cemeteries are highly structured and symbolic landscapes that have attracted comment. One scholar of conflicts in the twentieth century has argued such monumental and aesthetic treatments serve 'to enhance and redirect remembrance' away from the 'terrible consequences' of conflict.[96] The creation of such surroundings may present a challenge of remembrance, but one for the postwar generation. Veterans such as Matt Daley, Joe Dawson, Henry Ferri and Edwin Perry had no need of reminders: they carried their memories or carry them still. The challenge of memory exists for those who were not there, to understand how it was, to honour the terrible sacrifices of soldiers and civilians and the glorious results of liberation without glorifying war and conflict. Only then will we be able to draw the necessary lessons from D-Day and Normandy.

## Colleville 1944

FOX RED

FOX GREEN

EASY RED

Cabourg

Colleville - sur - M

Then and now – Colleville. (*NARA BIGOT Chart Map and Google Earth*)

Normandy
American
Cemetery

Google Earth

St Laurent 1944

0       500 METERS

L12
10
L10
L11
L9
EASY RED
WN 65
9
APPROXIMATE LOCATION OF AIR STRIP
L13
St Laurent-sur-Mer
L14
EASY GREEN
WN 66
les Moulins
WN 67
WN 69
L16
WN 68
DOG RED
12
L15
13
11
DOG WHITE
Hamel au Prêtre
L17
DOG GREEN
WN 70
L18

Then and now – St Laurent. *(NARA BIGOT Chart Map and Google Earth)*

APPROXIMATE LOCATION OF AIR STRIP

Saint-Laurent-sur-Mer

La Fraisnaie

Les Moulins

Les Fosses Taillis

**First** —
**Cemetery**
**Memorial**

Google Earth

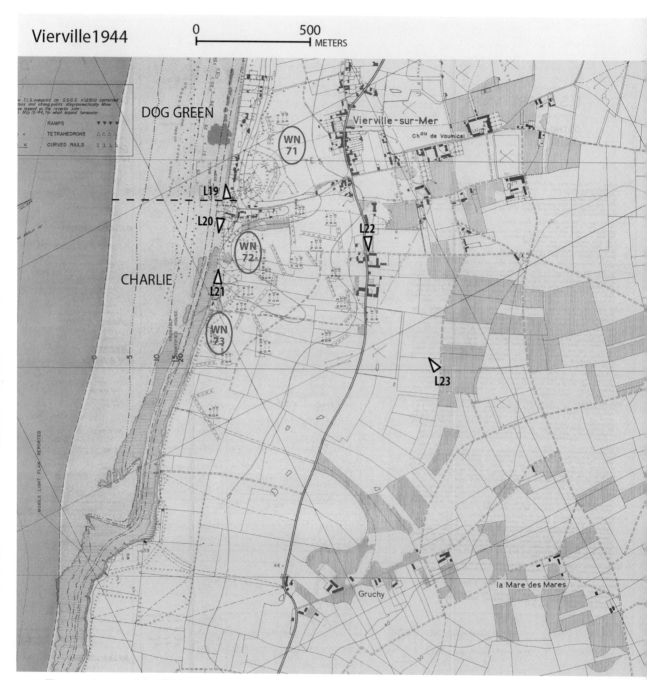

# Vierville 1944

0    500
METERS

DOG GREEN

WN 71

Vierville-sur-Mer

Ch<sup>au</sup> de Vaumicel

L19

L20

WN 72

CHARLIE

L21

WN 73

L22

L23

Gruchy

la Mare des Mares

Then and now — Vierville. (*NARA BIGOT Chart Map and Google Earth*)

(**Above**) Omaha Beach on 1 July 1944 from the former defensive position WN 60, located on the bluff above the beach where Richard Taylor photographed the displaced soldiers. Exit F-1 is shown in the foreground. (Image L1 facing north-west on Colleville 1944) *(NARA)* (**Below**) The modern view facing west from the same position.

(**Above**) WN 62 photographed in May 1946. The site was called 'Red Ball Hill' since Exit E-3 was a major route inland for supply trucks during the summer of 1944. The monument to the engineers has already been placed on the upper 76mm casemate. (Image L2 on Colleville 1944) (*NARA*) (**Below**) The modern view from near the Fox Green/ Easy Red boundary.

(**Above**) An early June 1944 image of the Ruquet Valley or Exit E-1 labelled 'Easy Green Beach St. Laurent sur Mer Airfield France'. A newly created air strip was located on the bluff to the left. (Image L11 on St Laurent 1944) (*NARA*)
(**Below**) The modern view facing the sea from approximately the same location.

(**Above**) A photograph by Todd on 7 June 1944 showing the 50mm casemate WN 65 on the west side of E-1. The casemate was reduced by the 2nd Battalion, 18th Infantry, late on the morning of D-Day. Many troops had landed in the vicinity since the traffic began moving through the exit by early afternoon. The sign 'Mars CP' denoted a command post location. The headquarters for the 1st Division was established nearby on the night of D-Day. Medical collecting and clearing companies from the 61st Medical Battalion established a station for wounded in the shelter provided by a nearby anti-tank ditch. (Image 10 on St Laurent 1944) (*NARA*) (**Below**) The modern view of the same casemate.

(**Above**) A view of the 88mm casemate and gun in WN 72 at the entrance to Exit D-1 on Dog Green sector near Vierville, recorded by Weintraub on 4 August 1944. The stepped screening wall served to shield the muzzle flash. This position provided enfilade fire along the beach and was one of two 88mm guns mounted in casemates; the other fired westwards from WN 61 on Fox Green sector. (*NARA*) (**Below**) The casemate was later converted into a memorial to National Guard troops such as the 29th Division, as seen in the modern view.

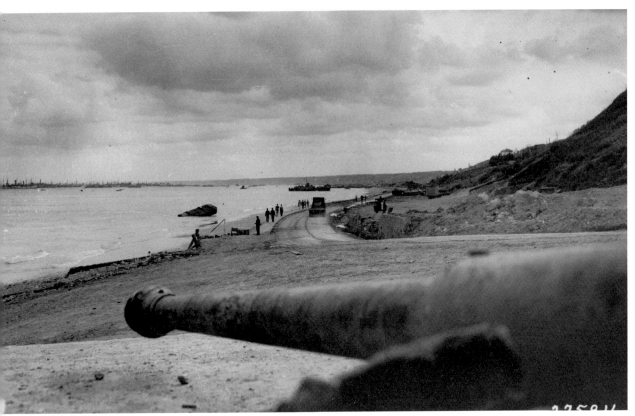

(**Above**) A view of Dog Green sector from the 88mm gun casemate at WN 72. Trichka recorded a series of views at the western end of Omaha Beach on 3 September 1944. A massive concrete wall blocked Exit D-1 on D-Day at the point where the road turned inland leading to Vierville. (Image L19 on Vierville 1944) *(NARA)* (**Below**) The modern view of Dog Green from the 88mm casemate at somewhat lower tide.

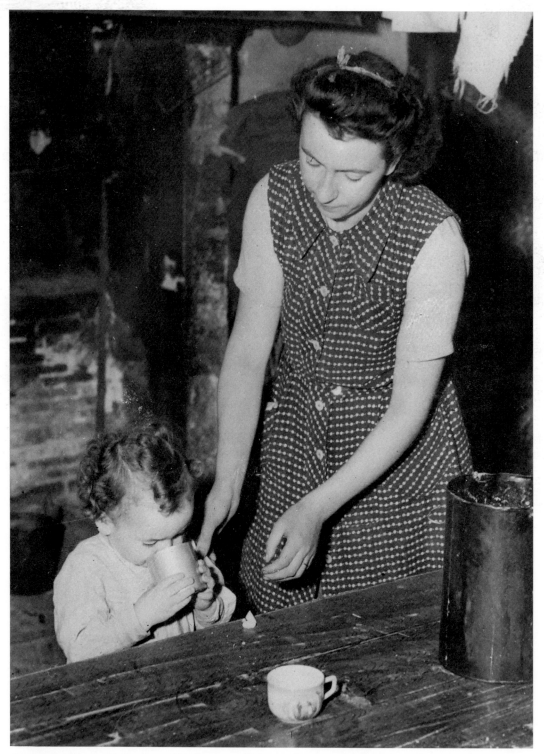

A young mother assisting her child drinking milk in a refugee camp. *(NARA)*

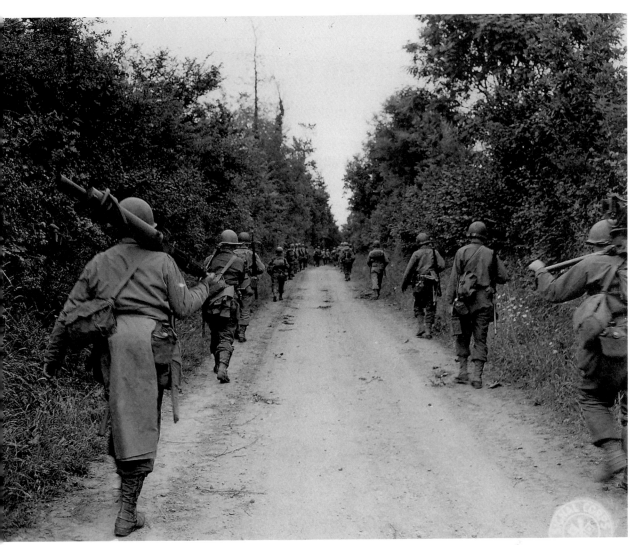

Collier captured an image of infantry moving south on 11 July on the long road inland to Saint-Lô. (*NARA*)

# Image Credits

NB: Page numbers are in **bold**. Any images not credited are from the author's collection.

## Chapter One: Preparations in England
**15** (top) NARA 111-SC-189702, (bottom) Robert Giannini and Patricia Daley Giannini; **16** (above left) Robert Giannini and Patricia Daley Giannini, (above right and bottom) Michael Perry; **17** (top) NARA 111-SC-189696, (bottom) NARA 80-G-252341; **18** (top) NARA 111-CPF-ETO44-1111, (bottom) NARA 111-CPF-ETO44-1222; **19** NARA 111-CPF-ETO44-1214; **20** (top) NARA 80-G-252146, (bottom) NARA 80-G-252126; **21** (top) NARA 80-G-252232, (bottom) NARA 111-SC-190375; **22** NARA 111-SC-190441.

## Chapter Two: Airborne Landings on the Cotentin Peninsula
**24** Ruppenthal, *Utah Beach to Cherbourg*; **27** Marshall, 'The Forcing of the Merderet Causeway'; **30** NARA 111-SC-377586; **31** NARA 111-SC-190367; **32** NARA 111-SC-377578; **33** (top) NARA 111-SC-377579, (bottom) NARA 111-SC-377580; **34** (top) NARA 111-SC-189996, (bottom) NARA 111-SC-190270; **35** NARA 342-FH-3A17430; **36** (top) Google Earth, (bottom) NARA 77-Army Map Service Sainte-Mère-Église 1944; **37** (top) NARA 342-FH-3A17432, (bottom) Google Earth; **38** NARA 342-FH-3A17431; **39** (top) Google Earth, (bottom) NARA 111-SC-320873; **40** (top) NARA 111-SC-320851, (bottom) NARA 111-SC-190286; **41** (top) NARA 111-SC-190122, (bottom) NARA 111-SC-190123; **42** NARA 111-SC-190294; **43** (bottom) NARA 111-SC-190231; **44** (top) Military History Institute 124A-12 Marshall Collection; **45** (bottom) Military History Institute 124A-3 Marshall Collection; **46** (bottom) NARA 111-SC-190347; **47** Military History Institute 124A-4 Marshall Collection; **48** NARA 111-SC-190348; **49** (top) NARA 111-SC-190403, (bottom) NARA 111-SC-320862; **50** (top) NARA 111-SC-190402, (bottom) NARA 111-SC-320864; **51** NARA 111-SC-190387; **52** NARA 208-Signal Corps-28940.

## Chapter Three: Landings on Easy Red and Fox Green
**60** NARA 26-G-2340; **61** (top) NARA 26-G-2342, (bottom) NARA 26-G-2337; **62** NARA 26-G-2343; **63** (top) Robert Capa © International Center of Photography/Magnum Photos, (bottom) Robert Capa © International Center of Photography/Magnum Photos; **64** NARA 26-G-2344.

## Chapter Four: The Photographs of Sergeant Richard Taylor (Fox Red Sector)
**69** NARA 111-SC-190682; **70** NARA 111-SC-189922; **71** (top) NARA 111-SC-189924; **71** (bottom) NARA 111-SC-189925; **72**, (bottom) NARA 111-SC-189910; **73** NARA 111-SC-320899; **74** (top) NARA 111-SC-192575, (bottom) NARA 111-SC-189915; **75** (top) NARA 111-SC-189916, (bottom) NARA 111-SC-189923; **76** (top) NARA 111-SC-189935.

## Chapter Five: Beach Landings and Views
**82** Shea, 'The Capture of Vierville'; **83** Shea, 'The Capture of Vierville'; **87** NARA 111-SC-400327; **91** (top) Bernard Lebrec, (bottom) NARA 111-SC-320901; **92** NARA 342-FH-3A17190; **93** (top) Google Earth; **93** (bottom) NARA 111-SC-189988; **94** (top) NARA 111-SC-189987, (bottom) NARA 111-SC-189986; **95** NARA 111-SC-920902; **96** NARA 80-G-421289; **97** (top) NARA 80-G-421287, (bottom) NARA 80-G-421288; **98** (top) NARA 111-SC-189899; **99** NARA 80-G-231580;

**100** (top) NARA 26-G-2966, (bottom) NARA 111-SC-206541; **101** NARA 342-FH-3A17165; **102** NARA 342-FH-3A17189.

## Chapter Six: Utah Beach and Coastal Defences
**107** (top) NARA 111-SC-320885; **107** (bottom) NARA 111-SC-190062; **108** (top) NARA 111-SC-190109, (bottom) NARA 111-SC-320894; **109** NARA 111-SC-190240; **110** (top) NARA 111-SC-190267, (bottom) NARA 111-SC-190233; **111** (top) NARA 111-SC-190064, (bottom) NARA 111-SC-190061; **112** NARA 111-SC-275765; **113** (top) NARA 111-SC-190117, (bottom) NARA 111-SC-190247.

## Chapter Seven: Soldiers, Prisoners and Civilians
**118** NARA 111-SC-320900; **119** (top) NARA 111-SC-189918, (bottom) NARA 111-SC-189928; **120** (top) NARA 111-SC-189929; **121** (top) NARA 111-SC-189930; **122** (bottom) NARA 111-SC-190245; **123** NARA 111-SC-189926; **124** NARA 111-SC-189927; **125** (top) NARA 111-SC-189919, (bottom) NARA 111-SC-189921; **126** (top) NARA 111-SC-189920, (bottom) NARA 111-SC-190258; **127** NARA 111-SC-190120; **128** NARA 111-SC-332023; **129** (top) NARA 111-SC-191890, (bottom) NARA 111-SC-190262; **130** (top) NARA 111-SC-190372, (bottom) NARA 111-SC-190265; **131** (top) NARA 111-SC-190259, (bottom) NARA 111-SC-190329; **132** (top) NARA 111-SC-190065, (bottom) NARA 111-SC-190116; **133** NARA 111-SC-191326; **134** NARA 111-SC-191454; **135** (top) NARA 111-SC-191875, (bottom) NARA 111-SC-192024; **136** (top) NARA 111-SC-191888, (bottom) NARA 111-SC-302866; **137** NARA 111-SC-190255; **138** NARA 111-SC-190253; **139** (top) NARA 111-SC-190287, (bottom) NARA 111-SC-190213; **140** NARA 111-SC-190212; **141** (top) NARA 111-SC-190424, (bottom) NARA 208-Signal Corps-30595; **142** (top) NARA 111-SC-191981, (bottom) NARA 111-SC-325937; **143** NARA 111-SC-332516; **144** (top) NARA 111-SC-191885, (bottom) NARA 111-SC-332514; **145** NARA 111-SC-332584.

## Chapter Eight: Advance to Cherbourg and Interior to Saint-Lô
**151** NARA 111-SC-190389; **152** NARA 111-SC-190328; **153** (top) NARA 111-SC-332029, (bottom) NARA 111-SC-332027; **154** NARA 208-Signal Corps-27972; **155** (top) NARA 208-Signal Corps-27966, (bottom) NARA 111-SC-332028; **156** (top) NARA 111-SC-332030, (bottom) NARA 111-SC-206555; **157** (left) NARA 111-CPF-ETO-442300, (right) NARA 111-CPF-ETO-442318; **158** NARA 111-SC-191982; **159** (top) NARA 111-SC-191986, (bottom) Bundesarchiv Bild 101I-721-0396-21; **160** (top) Bundesarchiv Bild 101I-721-0388-11, (bottom) NARA 111-Signal Corps-191627; **161** Bundesarchiv Bild 101I-721-0388-23A; **162** (top) Bundesarchiv Bild 101I-584-2159-07, (bottom) NARA 111-SC-368288; **163** NARA 111-SC-191444; **164** NARA 111-SC-191912; **165** (top) NARA 111-SC-332054, (bottom) NARA 111-SC-191662; **166** NARA 111-SC-191663; **167** (top) NARA 111-SC-211750, (bottom) NARA 111-SC-332055; **168** NARA 111-SC-191626; **169** (top) NARA 111-SC-412391, (bottom) NARA 111-SC-191892; **170** (top) NARA 111-SC-191628, (bottom) NARA 111-SC-191874; **171** NARA 111-SC-332946; **172** (top) NARA 111-SC-191876, (bottom) NARA 111-SC-192156; **173** NARA 111-SC-192000; **174** NARA 111-SC-192037; **175** (top) NARA 111-SC-192008, (bottom) NARA 111-SC-191809; **176** NARA 111-SC-192021; **177** (top) NARA 208-Signal Corps-31079, (bottom) NARA 208-Signal Corps-30983; **178** (top) NARA 111-SC-191997, (bottom) NARA 111-SC-332062; **179** NARA 111-SC-192004; **180** NARA 208-Signal Corps-29532.

## Chapter Nine: The Wounded
**187** (top) NARA 111-SC-190289, (bottom) NARA 111-SC-190229; **188** (top) NARA 111-SC-190464, (bottom) NARA 111-SC-206439; **189** (left) NARA 342-FH-3A18988, (right) Google Earth;

**190** (top) NARA 111-SC-190235, (bottom) NARA 208-Signal Corps-26385; **191** NARA 80-G-252726; **192** NARA 208-Signal Corps-31207; **193** (top) NARA 111-SC-206554, (bottom) NARA 111-SC-190306; **194** (top) NARA 208-Signal Corps-32428, (bottom) NARA 208-Signal Corps-29540; **195** NARA 111-SC-191440; **196** (top) NARA 111-SC-191441, (bottom) NARA 111-SC-325699; **197** NARA 111-SC-191241; **198** NARA 111-SC-191723; **199** (top) NARA 111-SC-325597, (bottom) NARA 111-SC-191829; **200** Bundesarchiv Bild 101I-722-0406-09A; **201** NARA 111-SC-192033

## Chapter Ten: The Dead and Their Cemeteries

**205** (top) NARA 26-G-2397, (bottom) NARA 111-SC-190601; **206** NARA 111-SC-320860; **207** (top) NARA 80-G-231417, (bottom) NARA 111-SC-190292; **208** (top) NARA 111-SC-320882, (bottom) NARA 111-SC-190368; **209** NARA 111-SC-190211; **210** NARA 111-SC-190392; **211** (top) NARA 111-SC-191896, (bottom) NARA 111-SC-191830; **212** NARA 111-SC-191882; **213** NARA 111-SC-325599; **214** (top) NARA 111-SC-247899; **215** NARA 111-SC-320876; **216** (top) NARA 111-SC-320855, (bottom) NARA 111-SC-192353; **218** (top) NARA 111-SC-572200, (bottom) NARA 111-SC-190826; **219** NARA 111-SC-191438; **220** (top) NARA 111-SC-275428, (bottom) NARA 111-SC-275429; **221** NARA 111-SC-191984; **222** (top) NARA 111-SC-244325, (bottom) NARA 111-SC-508608

## Chapter Eleven: Then, Now and Then

**230** NARA BIGOT Chart Map; **231** Google Earth; **232** NARA BIGOT Chart Map; **233** Google Earth; **234** NARA BIGOT Chart Map; **235** Google Earth; **236** (top) NARA 111-SC-206826; **237** (top) NARA 111-SC-243381; **238** (top) NARA 342-FH-3A17149; **239** (top) NARA 111-SC-190266; **240** (top) NARA 111-SC-275420; **241** (top) NARA 111-SC-275816; **242** NARA 208-Signal Corps-31118; **243** NARA 111-SC-191443

# Notes

1. Keegan, *The Face of Battle*, 72–4. Some of Marshall's conclusions such as the 'ratio of fire' estimate have proven controversial and later historians have called his research methods into question.
2. Wilmot, *The Struggle for Europe*, 265.
3. Shea, '29th Division on D-Day and in Normandy', 2–3.
4. Keegan, *Six Armies in Normandy*, 114.
5. Bennett, *Ultra in the West*, 71–4, 86–8, 102–4, 111-19
6. Fussell, *The Boys' Crusade*.
7. Ed Wright to Wendell Wilkie, 20 November 1943.
8. Ed Wright to Wendell Wilkie, 9 January 1944.
9. Gavin diary, 2 March 1944.
10. Gavin diary, 28 March 1944.
11. Gavin diary, 22 February 1944.
12. Gavin diary, 5 June 1944.
13. Hansen diary, 3 June 1944.
14. Bradley, *A Soldier's Story*, 234.
15. Gavin diary, 19 February and 18 March 1944.
16. Marshall, Comment on 82nd Division Operation, 4.
17. Marshall, Comment on 82nd Division Operation, 4–5.
18. Marshall, 'The Fight at the Lock', 23.
19. Marshall Neuville-au-Plain; 505th Parachute Infantry Regiment at Sainte-Mère-Église.
20. Marshall, Comment on 82nd Division Operation, 4–5.
21. 82nd Airborne debriefing conference, Sanford comments, 13 August 1944.
22. Gavin, *On to Berlin*, 115–6.
23. Marshall, Notes on the 325th Narrative; The Forcing of the Merderet Causeway at la Fière.
24. Marshall, *The Carentan Causeway Fight*.
25. Capa, *Slightly Out of Focus*, 139.
26. Hanson Baldwin in the introduction to *Danger Forward* used 'The Big One' omitting 'Red' commonly used today.
27. Bradley, *A Soldier's Story*, 154–6, 236–7.
28. Henry Ferri, interview 22 August 2014.
29. Beck et al., *The Corps of Engineers*, 324; Taylor *Omaha Beachhead*, 43–4. Perry Recommendation for Award 17 June 1944.
30. 1st Division G-3 Journal, 6 June 1944.
31. Capa, *Slightly Out of Focus*, 137.
32. 16th Infantry Comments and Criticisms on Operation Neptune June–July 1944 by Lieutenant Colonel Charles Horner, Captain Emerald Ralston and Major Charles Tegtmeyer.
33. Balkoski, *Beyond the Beachhead*, 288.
34. Bradley, *A Soldier's Story*, 236.
35. 'Meeting the Problem of Combat Exhaustion', 2 October 1944; Roberts, *What Soldiers Do*, 173–5.
36. Marshall combat interviews A/116th; Taylor, *Omaha Beachhead*, 46–8; Balkoski, *Omaha Beach*, 120–2; Goldstein, *New York Times*.
37. Shea, 29th Division; Taylor, *Omaha Beachhead*, 56–7.
38. Shea, 'Capture of Vierville', 6.

39. Shea, 'Capture of Vierville', 15; Bernage, *Omaha Beach*, 51, 53.
40. Shea, 'Capture of Vierville', 20; The D-Day Experiences of Company C, 116th Infantry.
41. Pogue interviews with John Thaxton and Walter Wilborn, 26 June 1944.
42. Daley interview, 1999.
43. Taylor, *Omaha Beachhead*, 83; Morison, *The Invasion of France and Germany*, 145, 147.
44. Hansen diary, 6 June 1944, 7.
45. Bach journal, 6 June 1944 in Shea 29th Division.
46. 505th Journal, 6 June 1944; Marshall, 505th Parachute Infantry Regiment at Sainte-Mère-Église.
47. Marshall, Cassidy's Battalion; 'The Fight at the Lock'.
48. Ruppenthal, *Utah Beach to Cherbourg*, 53–4.
49. Ruppenthal, *Utah Beach to Cherbourg*, 62–5.
50. Taylor, *Omaha Beachhead*, 89–92; Morison, *Invasion of France and Germany*, 125–9.
51. Ruppenthal, *Utah Beach to Cherbourg*, 66, 68, 104–5, 107–8.
52. Ruppenthal, *Utah Beach to Cherbourg*, 66–8, 104.
53. Carell, *Sie Kommen!*, 48–50.
54. Leleu, *La Waffen-SS*, 776.
55. Roberts, *What Soldiers Do*, 219.
56. Lilly and Le Roy, *L'armée américaine et les viols en France*, 120.
57. Roberts, *What Soldiers Do*, 226–9, 239–41.
58. Leleu, *Waffen-SS*, Table 14.
59. Ellis, *The Sharp End*, 286–7; Kennett, *G.I.*, 183; Leleu, *Waffen-SS*, 773, 776, 781.
60. Leleu, *Waffen-SS*, 781-4.
61. VIII Corps memorandum, 5 July 1944.
62. Roberts, *What Soldiers Do*, 53, 121.
63. *Ibid.*, 121, 130.
64. Wheatcroft, *New York Times Book Review*.
65. 115th A/A Report; Shea, 29th Division, 89–91; Pogue interview with M. Clift, 15 June 1944; Shea, The Third Battalion – 115th Infantry.
66. 505th A/A Report, 14.
67. 505th Journal, 16 June 1944 and A/A Report, 18, 21.
68. Hastings, *Overlord*, 163.
69. Balkoski, *Beyond the Beachhead*, 253–71.
70. Hastings, *Overlord*, 186–95.
71. Bradley, *A Soldier's Story*, 40-1, 322; FitzGerald, *Irish Guards*, 427 put the number at six.
72. FitzGerald, *Irish Guards*, 427; Bradley, *A Soldier's Story*, 41.
73. Tegtmeyer diary, 6 and 7 June 1944.
74. 643rd Annual Report, 5–6.
75. 61st Annual Report, 5–6.
76. *First US Army Report of Operations* VII, 65–6.
77. Marshall, 'Within the Perimeter', 2–3. The *First US Army Report* disagrees on this point, stating that jeep evacuations arrived at medical facilities near Utah Beach on 7 June.
78. *First US Army Report* VII, 65–6, 96.
79. Hansen diary, 7 June 1944.
80. *First US Army Report* VII, Appendices 11, 17 and 28; 643rd Annual Report, 15.
81. *First US Army Report* VII, 81, 85–6, Appendices 11 and 18.
82. Ellis *The Sharp End*, 167.
83. Ellis *The Sharp End*, 170-1.
84. *First US Army Report* VII, 77, 100.
85. 643rd Annual Report, 16.
86. *First US Army Report* VII, 96–8.

87. 643rd Annual Report, 16.
88. 16th Infantry Journal, 7 June 1944.
89. 506th Journal, 9 June 1944; 505th Journal, 11 June 1944.
90. Richardson and Allan, *Graves Registration*, 34; VDK, *German War Graves*, 9.
91. Richardson and Allan, *Graves Registration*, 34–5; VDK, *German War Graves*, 8.
92. Knischewski and Spittler, *Memories of the Second World War*; VDK, *If the stones could talk … Normandy*.
93. Abramson, *New York Times*.
94. Kingseed, *From Omaha Beach to Dawson's Ridge*.
95. Kennett, *G.I.*, 138.
96. González-Ruibal, 'A Time to Destroy', 257.

# References

**Army unit records, National Archives Record Group 112**

61st Medical Battalion Annual Report 1944 and History
643rd Medical Clearing Company Annual Report 1944

**Army unit records, National Archives Record Group 407**

*First US Army Report of Operations, 20 October 1943–1 August 1944*, Books I and VII.
VIII Corps 'Looting and Wanton Destruction of Property', 5 July 1944, copy in 505th Parachute Infantry files.
1st Division G-3 Journal.
5th Ranger Battalion Unit Journal.
16th Infantry S-3 Journal and After Action (A/A) Report by Major Carl Plitt.
16th Infantry Summary of Regimental Situation on D-Day, 6 June 1944 by Major Carl Plitt.
16th Infantry A/A Reports 3rd Battalion and Companies I–M.
16th Infantry Comments and Criticisms on Operation Neptune June–July 1944, specifically comments by Lieutenant Colonel Charles Horner, Captain Emerald Ralston and Major Charles Tegtmeyer.
18th Infantry 2nd Battalion A/A Report.
29th Division Combat Interviews, 'Meeting the Problem of Combat Exhaustion', 2 October 1944 by Major David Weintraub.
82nd Airborne Division Debriefing Conference for Operation Neptune 13 August 1944 comments by Lieutenant Colonel Terry Sanford 1/325th Glider Infantry (http://www.6juin1944).
115th Infantry A/A Report.
502nd Parachute Infantry History, 5 June–10 July 1944 and Action of 502-1 on D-Day.
505th Parachute Infantry S-3 Journal, 6 June–1 July 1944 ('Due to Action by the Enemy the Rest of the Unit Journal was Destroyed').
505th Parachute Infantry A/A Report, 5 June–15 July 1944.
505th Parachute Infantry, letter 'Maire de Sainte-Mère-Église au Monsieur le Commissaire du Gouvernement du General de Gaulle à Bayeux' undated.
506th Parachute Infantry Journal, 5 June–2 July 1944.

**Army unit records, National Archives Record Group 319 Entry P72 including Colonel Marshall files**

16th Infantry A/A Reports, 1st Battalion and Companies A-C, Companies E-G from 2nd Battalion.
16th Infantry Combat Interviews with Companies E-G and L.
116th S-3 Journal by Major Thomas Howie.
116th Infantry, A/A Report, 2nd Battalion.
116th Infantry, Combat Interviews with Companies A–D (including 'The D-Day Experiences of Company C, 116th Infantry'); Company E and 2nd Battalion summary Companies G–H; and Companies I–M.
Sergeant Forrest Pogue Interviews, mostly June 1944: Major Sidney Bingham, 2/116th Infantry, Sergeant John Thaxton and Technical Sergeant Walter Wilborn, F/116th Infantry, Captain Robert Walker, 116th Infantry, Major M. Clift, 2/115th Infantry.

Abramson J., 'Bush Speaks of Heroism and Sacrifice at Cemetery in Normandy', *New York Times*, p. A10, 28 May 2002.

Bach, S., Journal, 6 June 1944, Manuscript in Shea, J., 29th Division on D-Day and in Normandy, National Archives Record Group 319, Entry P72, 1944.

Balkoski, J., *Beyond the Beachhead. The 29th Infantry Division in Normandy*, Stackpole Books, Harrisburg, second edition, 1999.

Balkoski, J., *Omaha Beach*, Stackpole Books, Harrisburg, 2004.

Beck, A., Bortz, A., Lynch, C., Mayo, L. and Weld, R., *The Corps of Engineers: The War Against Germany*, Center of Military History, United States Army, Washington DC, 1985.

Benamou, J.-P., *Normandy 1944*, Heimdal, Bayeux, 1982.

Bennett, R., *Ultra in the West. The Normandy Campaign of 1944–45*, Charles Scribner's Sons, New York, 1979.

Bernage, G., *Omaha Beach*, Heimdal, Bayeux, 2002.

Bradley, O., *A Soldier's Story*, Henry Holt and Company, New York, 1951.

Capa, R., *Slightly Out of Focus*, Henry Holt and Company, New York, 1947, reprinted by Modern Library, 1999.

Carell, P., *Sie Kommen!* (*Invasion! They're Coming* translated from German by David Johnston), Schiffer Military History, Atglen, Pennsylvania, 1995.

Daley, M., oral history interview, 6 March 1999, OHPCN 0624, Reichelt Oral History Collection, Special Collections & Archives, Florida State University Libraries, Tallahassee.

*Danger Forward. The Story of the First Division in World War II*, Society of the First Division, Washington DC, 1947, reprinted by The Battery Press, Nashville, 1980.

Ellis, J., *The Sharp End. The Fighting Man in World War II*, Aurum Press Limited, London, 2009 (published 1980 by David & Charles, revised edition 1990 by Windrowe & Greene).

Ferri, H., oral interview, 22 August 2014, Army Heritage Center Foundation, Carlisle.

FitzGerald, D.J.L., *History of the Irish Guards in the Second World War*, Gale & Polden, Aldershot, 1949.

Fussell, P., *The Boys' Crusade. The American Infantry in Northwestern Europe, 1944–1945*, The Modern Library/Random House, New York, 2003.

Gavin, J., diary January 1944–September 1945, United States Army Military History Institute, Carlisle.

Gavin, J., *On to Berlin. Battles of an Airborne Commander 1943–1946*, The Viking Press, New York, 1978.

Goldstein, R., 'Ray Nance, Last of the Bedford Boys, Dies at 94', *New York Times*, 22 April 2009.

González-Ruibal, A., 'A Time to Destroy: The Archaeology of Supermodernity', *Current Anthropology* 2008, vol. 49 no. 2, pp. 247–79.

Hansen, C., diary, June 1944, United States Army Military History Institute, Carlisle.

Hastings, M., *Overlord: D-Day and the Battle for Normandy*, Simon & Schuster, New York, 1984.

Keegan, J., *The Face of Battle*, The Viking Press, New York, 1976.

Keegan, J., *Six Armies in Normandy: From D-Day to the Liberation of Paris*, Jonathan Cape Ltd, 1982, reprinted by Penguin Books Ltd, Harmondsworth, 1984.

Kennett, L., *G.I.: The American Soldier in World War II*, Charles Scribner's Sons, New York, 1987.

Kingseed, C., *From Omaha Beach to Dawson's Ridge: The Combat Journal of Captain Joe Dawson*, Naval Institute Press, Annapolis, 2005.

Knischewski, G. and Spittler, U., 'Memories of the Second World War and National Identity in Germany', in *War and Memory in the Twentieth Century* (eds M. Evans and K. Lunn), 239–54, Berg, New York, 1997.

Leleu, J.-L., *La Waffen-SS. Soldats politiques en guerre*, Ouverage publié avec le concours du Centre National des Lettres. Perrin, Paris, 2007.

Lilly, J.R. and Le Roy, F., 'L'armée américaine et les viols en France, juin 1944-mai 1945', *Vingtième Siècle. Revue d'histoire*, 2002/3 (no. 75), pp. 109-21.

Marshall, S.L.A., Combat Interviews 82nd Airborne, 1944. National Archives Record Group 407:
  'Comment on 82d Division Operation' during Operation Neptune.
  'Neuville-au-Plain Action of 3d Platoon, D Company, 505th Parachute Infantry'.
  'Notes on the 325th Narrative'.
  'Within the Perimeter'.

Marshall, S.L.A., Regimental Unit Studies 1944–45. National Archives RG 407:
  No. 1 'The Carentan Causeway Fight' (3rd Bn 502nd Parachute Infantry).
  No. 2 'The Fight at the Lock' (501st Parachute Infantry).
  No. 4 'The Forcing of the Merderet Causeway at la Fière, France' (3rd Bn 325th Glider Infantry and others).
  No. 6 '505th Parachute Infantry Regiment at Ste. Mère-Église'.
  Battalion and Small Unit Study No. 9 'Cassidy's Battalion' (1st Bn 502nd Parachute Infantry).

Marshall, S.L.A., *Night Drop. The American Airborne Invasion of Normandy*, illustrated by H. Garver Miller, Little, Brown and Company, Boston, 1962.

Morison, S.E., *The Invasion of France and Germany 1944–1945*, History of United States Naval Operations in World War II, Vol. XI, Little, Brown and Company, Boston, 1964.

Perry, E.R., Recommendation for Award of Distinguished Service Cross dated 17 June 1944 and signed by Major General Leonard Gerow (courtesy of Michael Perry).

Richardson, E.R. and Allan, S., *Quartermaster Supply in the European Theatre of Operations in World War II. Volume VII Graves Registration*, The Quartermaster School, Camp Lee, Virginia, 1948.

Roberts, M.L., *What Soldiers Do. Sex and the American GI in World War II France*, University of Chicago Press, Chicago, 2013.

Ruppenthal, R., *Utah Beach to Cherbourg*, Hist. Div., Department of the Army, Washington, 1947.

Shea, J., 29th Division on D-Day and in Normandy, National Archives Record Group 319, Entry P72, 1944.

Shea, J., The Third Battalion – 115th Infantry. An Outline of its Actions from D-Day to D+7 – its Attempted Crossing of the River Elle, National Archives Record Group 319, Entry P72, 1944.

Shea, J., 'The Capture of Vierville – D-Day Landings of 116th Infantry', National Archives Record Group 319, Entry P72, 1945.

Taylor, C., *Omaha Beachhead*, Historical Division, War Department, Washington, 1946.

Tegtmeyer, C., personal wartime memoir June 1944, National Archives Record Group 319 (http://history.amedd.army.mil/booksdocs/wwii/Normandy/Tegtmeyer/TegtmeyerNormandy.html).

Thompson, G. and Harris, D., *The Signal Corps: The Outcome,* Center of Military History, United States Army, Washington, 1991.

Volksbund Deutsche Kriegsgräberfürsorge, 'Normandy. The German War Graves Commission Working for Peace. German Military Cemeteries', ca. 2005 brochure available in Normandy September 2014.

Volksbund Deutsche Kriegsgräberfürsorge, 'If the stones could talk … Normandy', 2010 brochure available in Normandy September 2014.

Wheatcroft, G., 'Path of Least Resistence' review of *And the Show Went On* by Alan Riding, *New York Times Book Review,* 26 November 2010.

Wilmot, C., *The Struggle for Europe*, Harper and Brothers, New York, 1952.

Wright, E., Edward Wright Correspondence 1943–1944, Wendell Wilkie Papers. Courtesy, The Lilly Library, Indiana University, Bloomington, Indiana.

# Notes

# Notes

# Notes

# Notes